ESSA
JUNIOR

Published by
Lotus Press Publishers & Distributors

ESSAYS FOR JUNIOR CLASSES

Rajeev Bhatia

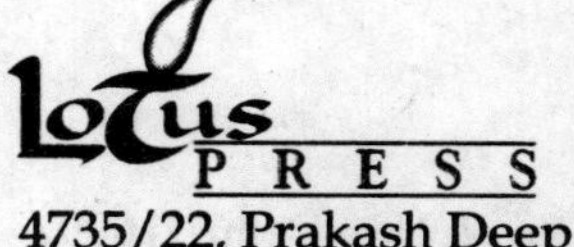

4735/22, Prakash Deep Building,
Ansari Road, Daryaganj,
New Delhi - 110002

Lotus Press Publishers & Distributors
Unit No.220, 2nd Floor, 4735/22, Prakash Deep Building,
Ansari Road, Daryaganj, New Delhi - 110002
Ph.: 32903912, 23280047, 09811838000
E-mail : lotus_press@sify.com
Visit us : www.lotuspress.co.in

Essays for Junior Classes

ISBN: 978-81-8382-244-2

Published by : **Lotus Press**, New Delhi-110002
Printed at : **Bharat Offset Works**, Delhi

PREFACE

Writing an essay is a good way to stimulate learning and critical thinking. Essay is an important method of assessment that will help children to display their skills and abilities which they possess.

An essay is a part of non-fiction and subjective write - up. The aim of junior level essays is to provide a vivid picture of a person, location, object and event or to describe the course of events from a subjective advantage point. The goal is to show superficial differences among different topics in various ways. In this book, we aimed at to make the children and give information on various sports, biography of famous personalities and on several of the topics.

Though, we desire to explore the maximum knowledge among the children, the main objective of this book is the among the children to increasing their educational level in an adequate manner.

–Author

CONTENTS

1. POLLUTION

Pollution is any substance or form of energy in dangerous concentration to harm living things or the environment. Pollution is created by individuals, communities and by industries that collect and dispose of pollutants improperly.

There are four kinds of pollutants, i.e., air, water, ground and energy.

Air pollution can be caused by carbon dioxide and automobile exhaust, combustion products from heating, power plants, radioactive particles, improper solid waste disposal, fires and chloro-fluorocarbons (CFCs). Polluting the environment means destroying the ozone layer. The ozone layer protects us from harmful ultra-violet rays and radiation. But too much air pollution on earth is slowing down the ozone's ability to re-build itself.

Water pollution occurs mostly when people overload the water environment with wastes. It is defined as contamination of streams, lakes, rivers, underground water, bays or oceans by substances harmful to living things.

Pollution makes streams, lakes, rivers and coastal water unpleasant to look at, to smell, and to swim in. Fish and shellfish harvested from polluted water may be unsafe to eat. People who ingest polluted water can become ill and if they're exposed for a long time, then cancer may develop or have children with birth defects.

To help, we need to learn about ways for disposing harmful household wastes so they don't end up in sewage treatment plants or landfills. We need to preserve existing trees and plants with new trees and shrubs.

Thus, life on earth is very fragile and it is extremely important that we should all realize the fragility of life by examining all the factors that affect it.

2. A YEAR OF CHALLENGE

Even though graduation from high school opens doors to a wide spectrum of choices, many students find that their lives are still tied to a list of expectations that they have carried since birth. When I was asked what I would do if I had an entire year free of all obligations, initially I had no idea. But then, I realized that there are a number of things that I would really like to do to fulfil all of my other commitments.

So, rather than spending an year abroad or dedicate myself to some cause, I would take time to spoil myself with life's little indulgences and accomplish a few things that I may or may not ever get a chance to do after college.

One of my favourite things to do is to go for mountain climbing, but since I always had to work during the summer I never had the luxury of spending more than a few days enjoying the beauty of the mountains.

Mountain climbing is an extraordinary experience because it gives me a great sense of accomplishment and many of life's lessons are revealed during the tedious journey to the top. For one, it teaches you to have faith. Just like with life's challenges, when you are suspended on a rock face by only a rope, you must learn to have faith in the rope, because like God, without it you will fall. Also, you must learn never to give up. As in life, the trail may become difficult, but if you are steadfast and find strength in the Lord, he will help you to reach the prize at the end, which in this case is the most spectacular view I have ever beheld.

3. GOALS

Goals are a very important part of our life. Everyone has dreams, hence setting goals helps them to fulfil their dreams. There are many types of goals, however, the two main categories are short-term goals and long-term goals. Another important part of having goals, is deciding which goals are more important than others.

Establishing priorities help to determine which tasks should be performed first, and how they affect one's goals. I set many goals for myself, however, the priority that place on individual's goal seems to come naturally. It is only upon further thought that I come to understand the process by which this takes place.

In general, all goals are very important to me. They help me to determine where I'm going and what I'll need to do to get there. Perhaps my ultimate goal, like that of many others, is a long-term pursuit of happiness. It seems that whatever goals I set, are steps taken towards the road of success and happiness.

I work hard now, to be happy later. Short-term goals, instant gratification and distractions are just small parts of the big picture.

Because I know that a little taste of happiness now, will keep me working towards happiness in the future. All things are relative however, happiness seems unattainable considering that one will always overlook their own achievements and be unhappy with what one doesn't have.

The first type of goal, the short-term goal takes little time, it is usually easy to achieve. These goals help to fulfil smaller desires as per the requirements. Many times these goals must be achieved like paying bills, doing homework and else many.

4. LOST WALLET

In my wallet, I generally keep personal items such as my license and some pictures. Among other things, I usually keep some money and certificates for stores. This summer, I went to the market with my family. I drove down there with my wallet and took it everywhere with me, as I always do. Well, when someone doesn't have pockets, then it is hard to keep their wallet right next to them at all times. I was carrying my wallet out from the hotel, along with my keys, and set both on top of the car.

When I figured out that I needed the keys in order to get in the car and turn it on, I took them off the top of the roof, leaving my wallet behind. I sat in the car, car door open, waiting for my father to come in, so we could not require to go to a driving area. Once he set in the car, without thinking, I closed the door and started the car. I had been driving about half a mile before I realized that my wallet was no longer on my body. Immediately, I pulled the car over, and the next hour or so was spent looking for my wallet.

All I could think about was what I would lose if I didn't find my wallet. While walking up and down the road that my wallet flew off on, my sister found my two Best Buy cards. That eased my mind a little. However, that was all we found of my favourite wallet. My family and I gave up after wasting an hour of finding nothing. Losing my wallet made me depressed for the rest of the day. I could not believe I did something so stupid.

Since that single event, I have lost my wallet two other times, none as serious as before. I have also lost something sincere to me by putting it on top of the car. However, I was fortunate enough to get it back. The carelessness of my misplacing have taught me a lesson, simply think before any act. This is something everyone is taught numerous times. Only now, it is easier for me to apply that to my actions. If I follow that idea, I could avoid future problems like this, preemptive caution. It took a scare like this for it to finally kick in to me.

5. MY INTERESTS

I am interested in anything that is interesting, though, I tend to gravitate towards computer, science and math.

Though I do not spend most of my daily time actively engaging in monastic exercises of personal study and reflection, or even in what would popularly be considered religious activity, I have determined to mold my entire life, moment by moment, in a way that is pleasing to God. This is my greatest interest.

The second-most done activity in my life is computing, as it is currently my job. I always try to spend some time off the clock exercising this interest, but if allowed free in the wild, it would probably take third place to the next interest: writing–I enjoy writing very much. My writing topics and style tend to match my electricity, though I enjoy the role of an essayist-poet most of all. I have written many instructional articles, though I have lately stayed away from them due to my over-exercise of that area of writing. I enjoy poetry and while few poets ever put bread on the table and write substantial amounts of poetry, I am not motivated by anything primarily for money and find poetry an expressive way to communicate things that prose is unable to.

When I have time to ride my bicycle, I do ride it willingly. At one point, I used to actively train and race, when I came out of obesity and worked more diligently on my physique than I am now. I still train, but you won't see me win any of the informal meets each Tuesday any more. But cycling provides another extra physical relaxation, despite the intensity of exertion, and I always feel refreshed, relaxed and motivated after a good ride.

6. MY DREAM

I picture myself at centre stage in most enormous and fantastically beautiful theatre in the world. Its walls and ceilings are covered in impeccable Victorian paintings of angels in the sky.

A single ray of light shines down upon my face, shining through the still, silent darkness and all attention is on me alone. The theatre is a packed house; however, my audience is not that of human beings, but rather the angels from the paintings on the walls come alive, sitting intently in the rows of plush seats.

Their warmth encompasses my body and I know at that moment that it is time to begin.

I open my mouth. From deep inside of my soul a melody flows out of my chest, off my tongue, and finally caresses my lips with the sweetest touch, and my song fills the air with a boldness like that of the glory of the angels.

The sound of my song is that of unfathomable wonder, a voice as sweet and smooth as the face of a child.

7. TEACHING

Have you ever set your mind to something and does not quit until you arrived at what you were striving for? For many people the answer to that question is no. Many people have dreams that they dream of for years and years, but never make the dreams a reality.

Teaching is a dream for me, and I would like it immensely if I could make my dream come true. I have various reasons that I would enjoy the profession of teaching, and some of the reasons include the desire I hold in my heart to work with young children, the numerous benefits that the career has, and to serve in my community.

My desire to work with young children plays an important role in my dreams of holding a teaching career. The many benefits that the teaching career has to offer is another factor of why I am fond of the idea of the career. One of the many benefits include the guaranteed vacation time that you have. I am fond of the idea of a definite vacation time that you have every summer.

Also having to work the same hours while my son is at school is important to me, because I can spend more family time together, if I become a teacher. The other benefits, such as the retirement and medical insurance, are valuable in my family life. The benefits that this profession offers seem near perfect in my lifestyle.

I enjoy having the influences on children to go on with life day-to-day; just being that older role model that offers advice when needed makes me feel delighted for what I have done.

8. FRIENDSHIP

There are many valuable things in life, but friendship may be one of the most important among all.

To live life without the experience of friendship is life without living. Human interaction is a necessity of survival, but developed friendships are an essential to the successful well being of anyone. Based upon the American Heritage Dictionary, the definition of a friend is a person whom one knows, likes and trusts. But to all, friendship has no defined terminology. The definition of a friend, and friendship, is based upon one's own notions. Many people look for different characteristics in friends, things that may be common in nature. There are many different types of friends that a person needs or wants. There are five different categories for these friends.

It is best in nature to recognize and appreciate various kinds of friends. The first type of friend in the friendship latter, is an acquaintance. This is the beginning to all basics, and deeper friendships. This is the person with whom, we only known on a pure.

The second type of friend is the soulmate. The name given to someone who is considered to be ultimate, true and eternal half of the other's soul. The third type of friend is the pen pal. They may or may not have met each other and may share either friendship or simply an acquaintance between each other. The fourth type of friend is spiritual friend who is a friend with a common interest, though they have more knowledge and experience than other and the fifth friend is fervency. Someone who tends to be a friend but actually is an enemy. So, one have to be careful while choosing a faithful friend.

9. HONESTY IS THE BEST POLICY

Probably honesty does pay in the long run. In business, for example, a man who deals straight forwardly with the public, who sells at fair prices, who gives good quality, and can be relied upon not to cheat, will generally establish a reputation that will be a fine business asset. People will be glad to deal with him; and though he may not make a fortune, he will have a sound and satisfactory business.

On the other hand, there is no doubt that success is often due to trickery, and great fortunes have been built upon dishonesty. Too many successful rogues have proved by experience that for them dishonesty had been the best policy. Of course, some of these people come to a bad end, and lose all they have gained by their lies; but many maintain their worldly success is more due to ability, lucky opportunities, and business cunning, than to honesty.

And many examples could be given of men who, from a worldly point of view, have failed because they have scrupulous honesty. A martyr who prefers to be burned at the stake rather than say what he believes to be false, may be a hero; but in the eyes of a worldly man, who thinks only of worldly success, he is a bad failure.

But if we look at such cases from the spiritual point of view – if we consider that truth and righteousness are far more important than wealth, rank and prosperity – then in the highest sense, honesty is the best policy. "For what it shall profit a man if he gain the whole world and lose his own soul?"

10. TALK ABOUT AN IDEAL HOUSE

An ideal house has four rooms with a well-furnished kitchen and modern bathroom facilities. The living rooms are comfortable. The furniture has been chosen with great care. The walls have been painted with soft colours to match the curtains, the materials of which had been bought from the best textile manufacturing company. Each room is fitted with audio system, so that one can enjoy programmes lying on bed. The drawing room is elegantly furnished with sofas, chairs and a central table. The walls are lined with built-in cupboards, a library to house well-chosen volumes by master novelists. There is a niche for the television and the room can be used for viewing programmes. All the rooms are air-conditioned and well designed.

The kitchen is beautifully done up. It is fitted with electric grills and things can be stacked neatly away in specially designed cabinets. It is provided with modern gadgets for grinding, pulverizing or cutting.

In front of the house there is an artificial pool with a fountain spray. One or two fish tanks are kept in the big porch to add the beauty of the place. There is a garage at the side of the house for car, cattle and poultry. In the backyard there are a few fruit bearing trees. On the margin of the house, there are some coconut trees. In front of the house there are certain bushes of croton and exotic plants. The well-kept lawn with luscious green grass is very pleasing to the eye. There is also a small playground for children with a swing.

A couple of hanging are fitted in the chandeliers in the drawing room showing rainbow coloured lights whenever light falls on them. There are a few selected pictures by masters in gilded frames.

Thus, one can feel surrounded by beauty and peace.

11. A JOURNEY BY TRAIN

When my father decided to take up a new appointment in the place where we live now, it was decided that we should travel by train. It was only then I discovered how pleasant a journey by train might be.

My father, mother and I boarded a train one afternoon.

The train was now moving quite fast. The first thing that impressed me was the beauty of the landscape. There were green valleys and tropical plants could be seen everywhere. In certain places there were tall grass also. All this reminded me of the geography lessons I had learnt in the classroom. Several palm-oil and rubber plantations could be seen now and then. Sometimes I saw a few houses here and there. I also saw many vegetable gardens at several places.

The train stopped at many stations and soon it became dark. But sometime later the moon appeared and the landscape looked romantic.

Inside the train, everything was interesting. Some restless passengers moved about aimlessly and their restlessness was amusing. Some were sleeping with their mouths wide open, into which some mosquitoes blundered while some were reading magazines and newspapers. Occasionally, the ticket-checker passed by. At one corner I saw two policemen keeping a close watch on a man who was hand-cuffed.

At every station a few passengers alighted from the train while a few boarded it. Whenever the train stopped at a big station, I saw a large number of people on the platforms, smartly dressed, and often smiling. As the train moved out, many waved their hands and the passengers too waved in response.

After we had passed several stations, I felt sleepy and closed my eyes.

When I opened them, I saw the dim light of the dawn. I looked outside and saw the mist-covered plants. The air was fresh, and some birds were flying about.

12. IMPORTANCE OF WATER

Since the beginning of time, water has continued to be important to all living things. Without water no one can survive. We may change our food according to the climate of a place but we can find no substitute for water. Man has always looked for pure fresh water to gratify his thirst.

Water not only quenches our thirst but it is also a source of food for us. From the sea we catch large quantities of fish and other creatures. We use water to irrigate our lands to produce crops. Many parts of the world are dry and barren because there is no water. People in such places lead a very hard life. Even the plants and animals find it a real struggle to survive. They can obtain water only by some means of ingenuity. Water also helps to increase the fertility of the land in several parts of the world. The alluvium that is brought down by rivers is very fertile. Even electricity, which has changed our lives completely, is produced by water-power in many countries.

Further, water is an important means of communication. We use waterways to carry our goods or trades. Water transport is cheaper than land transport and in many remote regions, rivers are the only means of communication. In many countries rivers are used to bring down timber from the hilly regions to the lower regions where there are timber mills. In this way much money is saved.

It is true; however, that water has also caused much destruction to life and property throughout human history. Heavy rainfall, swollen rivers and the angry waves of the sea have killed thousands of people and destroyed homes and crops. Yet, water is indispensable to life, and people everywhere are trying their best to bring water to places where it is scarce, to control its flow in times of floods and to make greater use of it.

13. GOOD MANNERS

Good manners play an important role in maintaining peace and goodwill in a community. A man who has good manners never hurt the feelings of others, and therefore he is on good terms with his friends, neighbours and also with the society. In this way he helps to keep peace in society.

But a man having bad manners has no respect for others. He uses words carelessly and behaves rudely towards others and causes a lot of ill-will and unpleasantness and hence suffers the most. Everyone avoids him and he is forced to live almost in isolation.

To live well in a society, money alone is not enough. We should also have good manners, for it is human nature to seek friendship; and friendship cannot be bought with money. Friendship with others makes life pleasant and it has to be earned through our own attitude towards others. If we are kind to others, they will be kind to us, and kindness is the essence of good manners. Bad manners not only drive away friends but also others, including our own family members.

On the other hand, a man having good manners has many friends. He commands the respect of all those who come into contact with him. He does not talk ill about others and never makes use of bad words. Even when he is provoked, he tries his best to use words in a way which will not offend others. He is also sympathetic towards the weak and ignorant and does not poke fun at the deformities and weaknesses of others.

If one's manners are good, one behaves well everywhere, even when one is away from the critical eyes of others. Only good mannered persons can live well in society.

14. THE IMPORTANCE OF AGRICULTURE

A human being is mainly a grain-eating animal. In Asia, most of the people eat rice. In Europe, North America and Australia, wheat is the main food crop. If rice and wheat cannot be grown, millet and other cereals are grown as food crops. Though men eat meat also they enjoy eating meat only when they take it together with rice or bread which is made from wheat. It is therefore clear that grains are the main source of man's food and grains are agricultural products.

Men, however, cannot survive only on grains. They need other foods to make his meals more palatable. Therefore, they learnt to grow vegetables, potatoes and fruits. Like grains, these things come from the soil. They have to be planted and grown with great care. As a result, men have made many experiments on soil for several centuries to increase their production of crops. Men have also learnt to consume dried leaves to refresh themselves. Tea and tobacco, the dried leaves of certain plants, have become very popular as sources of refreshment. Even coffee and cocoa are products of plants. Cotton, jute and other fibres are used to make cloth and several other things for our daily needs. All these plants have become very important in agriculture.

In some countries, agriculture is the main source of wealth. The rubber tree and the oil-palm in Malaysia bring millions of dollars every year. In Bangladesh, the jute plant is the main source of wealth. Similarly, in almost every country there is at least one plant which makes a great contribution to the economy of the country. We arrive at the conclusion that agriculture plays an important role in human world.

15. COLLEGE AND SUCCESS IN LIFE

It is very difficult to answer the claim that a person needs a university education to be successful in life because success in life means different things to different people. This essay starts by defining three different ideas of success. Following this, it looks at which types of success are dependent on a university education.

Success in life can be achieved in different ways. Many magazines and television programmes tell us that success means having a lot of money, having a fulfilling career, and being powerful. In contrast, most religious and spiritual organizations claim that success means finding spiritual happiness and being at peace with God and with yourself. Another idea of success focuses on relationships - being surrounded by people who love you and care about you, spending time with family and friends.

A university education can help you achieve some types of success, but it makes little or no difference to whether or not you are successful in other areas of life. Undoubtedly, a university education is essential if you want to have a career in a profession such as law, engineering, teaching, or medicine. However, you do not need a university degree to become a wealthy and powerful movie star, sports star or businessperson. In fact, a university education does not generally enable you to achieve spiritual happiness, or to have successful relationships with family and friends.

In conclusion, there are many different types of success. A university education may help you to achieve professional success in some careers. However, it will not help you to achieve success in other areas of your life such as your spiritual life or your relationships.

16. SHOULD PARENTS PAY?

Many crimes and social problems are caused by children. Despite the damage these teenage criminals cause, parents are not held responsible in most countries. This essay will discuss whether parents should be forced to pay for their children's crimes.

There are many reasons why parents should not be responsible for crimes committed by teenage children. First of all, teenagers today are independent. They often move out of the parent's house at 18 years of age or younger. They are expected to learn to take care of themselves and make their own decisions, and not like small children attached to their parents. Secondly, parents are working. They cannot watch their adolescent children all the time. A third point is that even children from good families can sometimes commit crimes. Parents should not be responsible if they have worked hard to raise their children properly.

However, because of many problems young troublemakers cause, I feel we should make parents responsible. Firstly, most juvenile crimes are committed by adolescents whose parents do not care or make any effort to control their children. If parents had to pay fines, they might make more effort. Another point is that even though the children may seem mature, they are not really able to make good decisions. Parents should be responsible for raising and teaching their children until they are fully grown. Furthermore, if children know that their parents will have to pay, they will think carefully before doing getting into trouble.

In summary, there are good reasons both for and against making parents pay for acts committed by their children. However, I feel strongly that if we want to reduce the number of such crimes, we need to make parents take more responsibility.

17. SHARING WITH A ROOMMATE

Many students are obliged to share accommodation with another student while in college. Sharing may seem awkward at first, but it may prove to be a very good experience. There are many positive aspects of sharing. New students are often far away from their families and friends, and may experience loneliness and homesickness.

Both may also be facing new challenges in their studies. Sharing offers companionship to people who might otherwise have to face these problems alone.

Furthermore, since college is not just about academic learning, sharing is an opportunity to develop communication skills so that a good atmosphere is established. Both students can learn from each other about new interests and explore new activities.

However, it is important to realize that your roommate does not have to be your best friend. In fact, the most desirable feature while living with someone else is respect for the other person's needs. Neither you nor your roommate will be right all the time.

In conclusion, I think that there are more benefits than disadvantages in having a roommate, but it depends on both dealing with concerns honestly and sensitively in order to make student life as happy as possible.

18. HOME-SCHOOLING

An increasing number of parents are deciding that home-schooling is the best option for their children. They are unhappy with the quality or depth of education offered in the schools, or has other reasons why they feel that traditional schools are not suitable for their children.

One reason is social factors. Parents believe that the good behaviour they have taught the child will be lost in school. Another reason is concern over the quality of schooling available. Schools frequently have large classes. They are often under-funded, and staffed by teachers without sufficient knowledge of their subjects.

Subjects such as the family's religion or language may not even be available in the school. Other parents may disagree with the aims of the school curriculum, preferring for academic, social or cultural reasons to keep their children separate.

Finally, some children with special desires may need particular parental care. However, there are many arguments in favour of sending children to conventional schools. The first is that the children will be exposed to other children. These children may represent either a cross-section of society or a narrow group, but in either case the children will interact with each other and develop social skills. A second point is that the children will learn to function outside the family. They will not be dependent on their parents for their educational, emotional and social needs. A third point is that the children will find it easier to integrate when they finish school, as they eventually will, when they start work or college. Overall, while many parents work hard to teach their children at home, conventional schools are still the right choice for most children. Schools are not perfect, but they seem to be a proven way of preparing our children for the real world.

19. A VISIT TO THE CIRCUS

Circus in town! It was all over the place, in posters, in newspapers, everywhere. The Russian Circus was in town. There was so much talk about it, on almost every lip. The whole city seemed so excited about it and so was I. I have always loved to go to circuses ever since I was a small child. I was three years when I first went to a circus.

The first time when I went to a circus, I experienced some kind of a psychic fixation. My mind, heart, body and soul - all were fixed on to the circus activities. I still remember the sight of bizarre characters walking to the tune of the circus music.

But everything is, of course, now, very different. The circus was performing today. It had disturbed my rhythm of life, although it was something I could not complain about. I had even skipped a meal in all the excitement and anxiety that took over me.

As we entered the main entrance to the circus, it first took us to a big menagerie tent where one could walk cage to cage and from pen to corral viewing animals from all the corners of the earth. I saw my first guerrilla here. The elephants might outnumber from a dozen to twenty and it was not unusual to find a giraffe, a rhino and a hippo on display along with the polar bears.

Walking ourselves through the menagerie, we found ourselves in a big mammoth canvas tent, almost as long as a football field and seating several thousands. Here the actual performance took place, and as always it was brilliant and fascinating. The trapeze artists took away the show. The antics of the colourful and jolly clowns was so very humorous. They made us laugh till our bellies hurt. The animals were next, the elephants, the tigers, the lions and not to forget the dashing polar bear in its snow-white coat. The acts had been dangerous and very brave of the trainers. Time just flew by. The show came to an end. We all went back home happily.

20. THE SCHOOL GARDEN

The school garden is fun and important for the school because it brings us closer to nature. After you plant the vegetable or flower you feel that you've brought something to life, it feels really good. Also, when you see kids in the salad bar enjoying the vegetables you have probably planted, your emotion is great inside. You planted that vegetable and now that student is delighted to be eating it.

Another reason the school garden is fun is that kids who get bussed in from the city may not have a yard for gardening. They'd have that sensation too. They might even be more touched than the kids who live in the area around that kind of nature all the time.

I think the school garden was a wonderful idea and I hope you do, too.

29. WHEN IT RAINS IT POURS

As I sit near a window, suddenly a drop of rain falls over me and I feel a shade of darkness overcoming my side. I walk outside to feel it falling on me. As I lift my face towards the heavens to feel it falling on me, I have this dark feeling of being dried.

Rainy days and nights make me feel sad inside. I get depressed and want to stay in the house in my bed. Whenever it rains I usually come downstairs and look out of the window, only to see if my car is still in front of my door. As I stare at the sky, I think to myself, it's going to rain all day. But still, I thought, the sun could shine anyway, bringing with it the spring flowers that smell so lovely, the green grass, the blue sky, and the white clouds. Oh well, just a thought. I close my curtains and go back upstairs, I get back into bed and try to sleep.

Sleep eludes me because I am thinking about things like is life, death, and money. It begins to pour and as the rain falls harder and heavier, I feel myself beginning to fall asleep. Rain is like life, it comes and stays a while. Rain is like death, when it's time to stop it knows. Rain is also like money, when you have a lot of it, it pours. I dream of the day when the rain will go away, but until that day, I will listen to its drops on my window pane.

30. A DAY AT THE PARK

A couple of months ago I went to the park with my nephew. I remember the day like yesterday. The weather was cool and clouds were overhead. I sat by myself and watched him playing and watched everything happening around me. I wasn't expecting to find so many interesting things just watching people, but amazed at what I did discover. Children were all over the place and were wearing coats that had their favourite characters on them.

A girl had purple mittens with a teletubby on them and a boy had a blue coat with Thomas the Train on it. One small boy with green eyes had a hat with a ball on the top. There were only two mothers at the park and seven children not including a baby by the side of one of the mothers. The baby was asleep and was bundled up in two blankets, one pink and one had bunnies on it. The children were all playing a game of tag and were out of breath from running around.

One of the boys involved in the game fell down and began to cry. His mother broke away from conversations to tend to the need of her son. After a few minutes he was fine. While that was going on, the other children discovered that when they went down the slide it shocked them. They screamed with delight every time they went down the red plastic slide. After a while they started another game of tag.

The kids ran as fast as they could. They would kick up wet sand all over their backs as they ran. Before I knew, it was time to leave as my nephew and I walked back to my car, the thought of being a kid again would be great. All in all, the park was something that I never thought that I would enjoy so much, but I found it to be very interesting.

31. PLANTS

Plants are the basis of the food pyramid for all living things and other plants. They have always been very important to people, not only for food, but also for clothing, weapons, tools, dyes, medicines, shelter and many other purposes. Plants are beneficial for both human beings and animals. We eat many different types of plants such as fruits and vegetables in our day-to-day life. We also use plants for our herbs. Plants are also used to manufacture many different products such as shampoos, rubber, paper, and camera film. In some countries, fermented sugarcane is used instead of gasoline.

Animals use plants in many different ways also. They eat many fruits and other plants. Many animals use plants for shelter. Plants also provide animals with protection from predators. The destruction of different plants sometimes leads to animals becoming endangered or extinct. The basic structure of plants consists of roots, stem, leaves, flower and fruit or seeds. A flower is the part of the plant that makes the seeds. The main parts of a flower are the carpels and stamens. These parts are often found in the centre of the flower. There are egg cells in the carpel and pollen cells in the stamen. All flowers have four basic parts: sepals, petals, carpels, and stamen. Different flowers have different numbers and shapes or these parts.

Most plants can be divided into one or two general categories: herbaceous or woody plants. Herbaceous plants have soft stems, while woody plants are tree-like. Herbaceous plants produce completely new stems each year. The approaching cold weather causes the newstems to die back to the ground. Some herbaceous plants survive periods of cold by forming underground bulbs, or tubers used for food storage. Many herbaceous plants complete their life cycles within one growing season and the whole plant dies, even the roots. These are the annual produce seeds that will form new plants the next year. Land plants are divided into two groups based on whether they have vascular tissues or not. All nonvascular plants are placed in one division. There are nine divisions of vascular plants. These are divided based on whether they form seeds or not.

32. SPECIAL EVENT IN MY LIFE

A Mother's Love as the years go by, I have encountered many rememberable moments from my first horse to the terrible car accidents. No matter if, it was good or bad times, nothing can or could surpass to compare the gift of becoming a mother.

There are so many memories wrapped in these packages of happiness, joy, and even times of fear knowing they don't come with instructions, but to learn as time goes on. From the first moments as a mother when coming into my world was like a new beginning of the chapter of life. All my worries and fears of becoming a mother had been washed away, I knew that moment of time life wasn't going to be the same. I was going to take life day by day and enjoying with my new family and was not concerned about the small details that life brings.

My life has become complete, I feel as though with this fresh start that myself as one can complete my dreams and hopes to a better future for us. As the long nights drag on to days and months of studying go by, I feel a moment of quitting, then I watch them both sleeping without a concern in the world only wanting to keep their image of the safe and peace of theirs dreams to come true.

Each day watching them grow brings me back to memories of my childhood. How your birthdays seemed almost like the best day compared to Christmas morning, and knowing that my children are feeling and imaging those same thought as I did so long ago. The hours go by as though they are seconds, the seasons flash past as though there is no end. One moment, to look back on my past of those special times and know it isn't over because I have my children to relive those special times all over again.

33. THE COLLEGE LIFE

The College Life Schedules are the difficult thing to balance. A person must find the time to complete a number of tasks in a day. A normal adult may have time to get everything done and still have time to spare. The normal college student on the other hand is constantly on the go. College students have busy schedules that include working, studying, and socializing. Some college students work. How else are they going to have the money for all those late night pizza deliveries? Part time employees usually eat on the road on the way from school to work. They work about 5 or 6 hours a day and then head home tired and ready for bed.

Maybe not every night but usually there is some kind of paper to be written or chapter to be read. Full time college students that are also full-time workers have to plan everything out in order to make the time to get everything done. One of the things most college students don't make time for is housework. They often wait until everything is dirty to start the laundry. Dishes are another thing that tend to pile up. Breakfast, lunch, and dinner plates and glasses add up after a week. College students must find time in their busy schedules to study. In order to keep up they must do daily assignments.

Reading every night helps to prepare for the exams. Taking notes in class and out of class are also necessary. Students also have exams at the end of the semester that require hours of studying. Waiting until the last minute and then cramming it all is often a final resort. Many students who have kept up just go over and recall the information. All students must find time to study in order to pass. To escape from studying and working college students are known for socializing. They may help out in service clubs. Visiting a nursing home can be relaxing and comforting for both people. Weekends are busy times for dance clubs in college towns. College students go to clubs for fun. Clubs can be a good place to make new friends or to meet up with old ones. To help relieve stress there is nothing like having a long talk with a good friend. College students are under a great deal of stress. They must manage their time wisely. As one can see their schedules are busy with working, studying, and socializing.

34. GOOD TEACHER

A good teacher can be defined as someone who always pushes students to do their best while at the same time trying to make learning about interesting as well as creative things. A positive or negative influence from a teacher early in life can have a great effect on the future of a child. Teachers, especially at the elementary level, must be very creative with their teaching styles. Not every child learns the same way, nor are they interested in the same things.

At the elementary level, children are always learning and sometimes have very little knowledge. When I was in kindergarten, I can remember playing at the different stations in the classroom.

A teacher who is constantly looking for the best possible work from the child will force the child to try his or her hardest in order to please the teacher. Going along with this idea is the whole idea of the teacher being interested in the subject matter. If the students know that the subject they are studying is something that greatly interests the teacher, they will be motivated to try their hardest in order to please the teacher. My ninth grade science teacher is the best example of this type of teacher. I was only in her class for about a month or so but it was probably the most interesting I have ever been in science in my entire life. Whenever she would present ideas about prehistoric man, her eyes would light up and she would get so excited that I would be forced to listen to whatever she had to say. Everyone had told me that she was a hard teacher but she never treated me that way. She had "done her homework" so-to-speak and was very knowledgeable about the subject matter.

35. WHY SOME STUDENTS CHEAT?

Nowadays there are many popular ways for students to cheat in exams. Some students take their notes into the examination rooms.

There are three main reasons why some students cheat in exams: being afraid of failure, having no ability, and wanting to take risks. Being afraid of failure is the most important reason for some students to cheat in exams. Some students think that if they fail in the exams, they will have a lot of following problems. For example, their parents will complain them about bad grades, their friends will look down and laugh at them, and they guess that the light of their educational futures will be darker too.

They will get stressed if they cannot do the exams as well as they hope and will lead them to cheat in exams. Some students just want to show off to their friends.

Without thinking thoroughly, they try to show their dishonest tricks in the examination rooms. These students probably think that cheating in exams is challenging and makes them cooler. Besides, they will get incredibly good grades if they succeed their cheating plans too. Therefore, to dare the punishments, some students cheat in exams for their pleasures.

Inconclusion, there are many reasons for students to cheat in exams, being afraid of failure, having no ability, and wanting to take risks, including the reasons which I did not state. And until today, we still cannot guarantee that there are ways to help students stop cheating. However, to those who are thinking to cheat the exams, you should think about the punishments, too. No matter what your reason is. Does it worth for being caught and got punished from both university and society? You all know the answer. Although you are not smart enough to have excellent grades, you should be proud of yourself that you try to get good grades by your own abilities, not cheating.

36. CAUSE AND EFFECT OF READING BOOKS

The ability to read is highly valued and very important for social and economic advancement. One of the effects that reading have on an individual, is the ability to understand more terms or words, over a period of time.

Children who are successful readers tend to exhibit progressive social skills. Having confidence in reading only comes from the daily practice of reading. One good way to accomplish the task of reading daily is through books. Reading books can develop a person's comprehension by learning new words. The easiest way to do this is to look up words in the dictionary that are not understood when they are read, for the first time. Writing these words down and reciting them aloud also help to establish them in memory.

The second effect that reading books has is vocabulary growth. Along the same lines of comprehension, the growth of vocabulary is also very important. Having a large vocabulary is not only impressive but useful in many areas of public speaking. Many different words have the same meaning, or as they are more commonly referred to, are synonyms. Looking for a word into the dictionary, one might be surprised to realize that they already know the meaning of the word. By cross-checking these words and learning the different synonyms to them, a vocabulary is being established. As a result of reading books over a period of time, a learning process is formed.

In summary, although only two effects are mentioned within this essay, there are great many benefits to be gained from reading books. It is proven that in this technological society, the demands for higher levels of literacy are creating unfavourable consequences for those who fall short. This is even more of a reason to get into the habit of reading books. Sharing books with a child is an active approach to the learning of lifelong language skills and to ensure future success with unforgettable quality words.

37. CHILDREN AND INNOCENCE

Children are born with the capacity to learn. Hate, envy, racism, selfishness; these traits are not instinctive, rather, they are learned. It does not matter where anti-social traits are initially experienced, whether it is found in the home, or school, or even in the nursery, the results are the same.

Children that are exposed to violence at an early age could have a propensity towards violent behaviour as they mature. Children must be shown that violent behaviour is not acceptable, and traits, such as compassion, are acceptable. Too many children today are left alone or unsupervised by guardians and parents. In today's society, it is a common trend for both the mother and father to work. Young children are many times left in the care of schools, friends, neighbours, and relatives. In these cases children behave in ways that imitate real life.

Children observe violence on television, at their school, or at home. According to a child, a violence is an acceptable behaviour because it is observed as being acceptable. It is imperative that young children are guided and taught the differences between right and wrong.

In a perfect society, this is all well and good. Unfortunately, perfect societies do not exist. The first five years of a person's life is sometimes referred to as the "age of innocence." Too many children today have never experienced the age of innocence. These children more often become adults with developed undesirable anti-social behaviours. A very high percentage of violent adolescents were found to have come from a disturbed and sometimes violent home life. When these same adolescents were asked if they could recall happy moments in early childhood, most could not recall any. Most certainly, the violence seen on television, in films, in newspapers and periodicals only amplified the acceptance of violent behaviour. Society must start with the newborn generation, and continue working with each successive newborn generation, until instances of violent behaviour begin to subside.

38. CLOUDS

I've opened the curtain of my east window above the computer and I sit now in a holy theatre before a sky-blue stage. A little cloud above the neighbour's trees resembles Mohan's nose for a while, then becomes amorphous as it slips on north. Other clouds follow, big and little and tiny on their way towards whereness. Wisps of them lead or droop because there must always be leading and drooping.

The trees seem to laugh at the clouds while yet reaching for them with swaying branches. Trees must think that they are real, rooted and that perhaps the clouds are only tickled water which sometimes blocks their sun. But trees are clouds, too, of green leaves--clouds that only move a little. Trees grow and change and dissipate like their airborne cousins. And what I am, a cloud of thoughts and feelings and aspirations? Don't I put out tentative mists here and there? Don't I occasionally appear to other people as a ridiculous shape of thoughts without my intending to? Don't I drift toward the north when I feel the breezes of love and the warmth of compassion? If clouds are beings, and beings are clouds, are we not all well advised to drift, to feel the wind tucking us here and plucking us out there?

Are we such rock-hard bodily lumps as we imagine? Drift, let me. Sing to the sky, I will. One in many, are we? Let us breathe the breeze and find therein our roots in the spirit. I close the curtain now, feeling broader and fresher. The act is over. Applause is sweeping through the trees.

39. FROZEN

Deep inside I was glad that I was chosen, outwardly cool, yet within I was frozen, it was sudden death match and I have to be bold. But a teammate did not do as he was told, he made the kid squeal like rat and I watched the opposing kid get pinned on the mat.

The crowd cheered, the team jumped for joy. Everyone surrounded the heroic young boy, I too cheered so no one would see, what I really felt was, it should have been me! Disappointment, anger and looking to blame. Did I miss my dream chance at fame? Nature's tears, the pounding rain cruelly mimic my resounding pain. Opaque clouds conceal her soul but mine is open, a bottomless hole.

That never heals, can never be cured, love dies inside, so rest assured, I shall no longer flood the land with endless droplets wiped by hand. Suddenly the horizon brightens hope and fear in my heart heightens. The myth of the clouds with the silver lining breaks the spell that was once confining. For now I feel my spirits rise as nature itself answers my cries. No longer shall I mope and mourn for he has mended my heart that was torn.

40. THE INTERVIEW

On early Friday afternoon, roughly one year ago, I was summoned to the conference room, that is, in the back of the building. I approached the conference room and opened the door with some hesitation, only to find my peers sitting at the conference table. All were staring at a new candidate that was there to be interviewed.

I looked across the room to see a man dressed in a pin stripe suit with creases that would make a military man proud at inspection. Although he was only of medium height and projected to be 10 feet tall. He had a confidence that seemed to fill the room and everyone felt it.

I approached him to welcome him with a handshake and I could feel his strength and positive attitude. Names were exchanged and he waited until I sat down before taking his seat. My peers and I were interviewing for a position that would involve all of us working together as a team. Questions were asked about his background, and he would use analogies to draw a clear picture with every answer. I felt as though I was watching television being able to see the answers in which he was so diligently giving.

Each of us sat captivated by the way he narrated his answers. Questions continued to flow back and forth. He made the pitch and sold us all. You could see by my fellow peers demeanour that this individual had an accepting audience, yes we had finally found the individual needed to fulfil the role required. At the end of this enthralling interview I opened the door for our candidate to leave. I shook his hand, and with a look of respect and acceptance he gladly accepted with a firm hand shake. He then said with a smile I hope to hear from you soon.

Today he sits diagonally across the room from me. He is very respected and a team player. His contributions have helped us all and this company.

41. EDUCATION: LOSING ITS VALUE

Today, it seems to be universally accepted that increased education is a good thing. Thousands of colleges and millions of students spend vast amounts of time and money in chasing pieces of paper. But are these qualifications valuable? This essay will discuss whether education has been devalued.

Supporters of education (usually teachers or educators, or those in the business of education) say that increased levels of education will open doors for students. Certificates, diplomas, and degrees are held up as a status symbol, a passport to a private club of money and power.

However, the truly powerful are not those with degrees, but people who stand back and look at what is really important in life. These people are found in every part of society. Like many brilliant people, Einstein was a weak math student. Like many successful businessmen, Bill Gates never completed college. Like many inventive and creative people, Edison never went to school. The greatest religious teachers don't have letters after their name. Similarly, many of the world's political leaders do not have master's degrees or doctorates. These are the people who shape our lives, and they are too busy with real life to spend time in the paper chase.

Students in college are being sold as an illusion. They are made to believe that self-understanding and society approval will come with the acquisition of a piece of paper. Instead of thinking for themselves, and finding their own personality and strengths, they are fitted like square pegs into round holes, in so-called professional jobs.

The role of education is to prepare masses of people to operate at low levels of ability in a very limited and restricted range of activities. Some of these activities are perhaps more challenging than the assembly lines of the past, but the ultimate purpose is equally uninteresting. More worryingly, despite the increased level of education, people are still not genuinely expected to think for themselves. In fact, the longer years of schooling make the job of brainwashing even easier.

42. WHO LEARNS FASTER : CHILDREN OR ADULTS?

Small children seem to learn very quickly, while adults sometimes appear to lose the ability to grasp new subjects such as languages, music, games, or computer programs. In this essay, I will discuss whether children or adults make the best learners.

It is undoubtedly true that children seem to learn very quickly. In just a few years, they can learn how to play a musical instrument, speak one or even two new languages, and deal with many subjects at school. They even have time for sports and hobbies, and become experts in their favourite pastimes. However, how much of this is social pressure and how much is genetic? I am convinced that while children's brains have a natural ability to absorb new information as part of their developmental growth, much of their achievement is because of social pressure. Schools force them to take many subjects. Parents force them to practice new sports or to learn music. Even their playmates force them to become better at computer games or to read Harry Potter novels faster. In summary, children may enjoy learning, but their environment also is a big motivating factor.

Adults, on the other hand, are supposed to be poor learners. However, I disagree with people who say that adults cannot learn quickly. Adults have many skills that compensate for the decline in the ability of the brain to grasp and remember new material. They can organize their learning by setting times for reading or practice. They can build on skills and experiences they already know. Adults usually cannot learn to do ballet or to play the violin, but even despite these physical challenges, their motivation can often be higher than an individual child. Unfortunately, society does not encourage many adults to learn. People are busy with families and work, and some adults may feel that further learning is pointless, since they have already achieved many goals at work or in their personal life.

In conclusion, I feel that we cannot generalize about children or adults being better learners. It depends on the situation and the motivation of the person, and the level of enthusiasm he or she has for learning.

43. MICROWAVES

While microwaving Water to Heat it Up!!! Please be aware of the following information if you or someone you know, is a person that uses a microwave oven to heat water. About five days ago a 26-year old man decided to have a cup of instant coffee. He took a cup of water and put it in the microwave to heat it up (something that he had done numerous times before). I am not sure how long he set the timer for but he said he wanted to bring the water to a boil. When the timer shut the oven off, he removed the cup from the oven. As he looked into the cup he noted that the water was not boiling, but instantly the water in the cup blew up into his face.

The cup remained intact until he threw it out of his hand, but all the water had flown out into his face due to the buildup of energy. His whole face is blistered and he has 1st and 2nd degree burns to his face, which may leave scarring. He also may have lost partial sight in his left eye. While at the hospital, the doctor who was attending on him stated that this was a fairly common occurrence and water (alone) should never be heated in a microwave oven. If water is heated in this manner, something should be placed in the cup to diffuse the energy, such as a wooden stir stick, tea bag (without the metal staple), etc. It is, however, a much safer choice to boil the water in a teakettle. Please pass this information on to friends and family. Take care, all!

44. COMPUTERS IN SOCIETY

The use of computers in and out of school has made improvements in the way we learn different things. Furthermore, the use of computers in the home has extended the hours we can learn at a higher level without the environmental pressures of school or work, thereby improving the way we learn. Also, the use of computers has expanded our choices for entertainment.

The ability of the computer to link a person with others from far away places where conversations without inferences are sparked and ideas are exchanged internationally, is a popular selection for millions of people everyday as a choice for entertainment. I also think the working environment where computers are used is becoming more and more diverse. As an example, in developed countries farmers have computers in their tractors hooked up to GPS (Global Positioning Satellite) systems that not only tell them where to spray their pesticides but are programmed to take care of the task for them as they drive along–all because a digital image from a satellite some 23,000 miles away saw too many bugs in a certain part of one of his fields is very diverse.

Another way diversity is becoming the norm with the influx of wireless technology, that it has made is possible for mobile "laptop" computers to be linked up to a global network, not just for the mobile office, but for the person sitting on a beach on some south pacific island and still being able to attend a meeting in London is diversity at the extreme. Computers are really fascinating and becoming more and more amazing day by day as they weave their way into our lives. Don't think that you are not knowledgeable about the computer. You really know that appropriate knowledge of computers and its usage is not possible. From waking in the morning, to the food at the dinner table, to the movie afterwards, computers have influenced the way we live and will continue to do so for the foreseeable future.

45. WORK AND SCHOOL

Many people have busy lives, especially someone who has to juggle more than one task per day. The people in particular that I am talking about are college students. How some of us have jobs and some need jobs that help to keep us in school with an appropriate amount of money provided.

The tough part is that we have to spend most of our time on school which leaves very little time for work, even though we do have to work to make a decent amount of money. So, since work and school are apart of everyone's life, either if you just work or go to school, they both involve a good amount of your life and time. On the other hand, going to work and school at the same time can make it tough to concentrate on one even though you have to do both. One thing that students need to know is time management. It is o.k. to work and go to school, but each person has to give a demanded amount of time for both.

Many students, like myself, like to work, and we will sometimes do that more than school. In contrast we have to give the same if not more time to school. The reason for this is because probably the job you are working on now is not going to get you that high paying job that you will be looking for when you are out of school. Students have to remember that and not put all of their time into work.

Some people like myself feel obligated to work more since we have more time out of class than we did in high school. Another thing that I notice myself doing is going to work right after school which leaves only a little time to do homework usually late at night. Most of the time that homework is not get done because we are so tired from working all night. So, we will put it off until the night before it is due. I, personally as a procrastinator, will put things off until the night before it is due and start it then. Everyone needs to know the value of time management. Not being able to put the right amount of time to the most important thing is not a good habit.

46. BECOMING A POLICE OFFICER

I respect police officers and always wished to become as strong and hard as them. Police officers help to protect citizens and their property, maintain public peace, prevent and detect crime.

In their daily work, police officers perform many duties ranging from enforcing the law and apprehending criminals, to controlling traffic and arbitrating domestic disputes.

Police work does not always involve a physical act of protection or the apprehension of a lawbreaker. It also involves activities such as crime prevention activities, helping victims of crime, working with community groups to identify and solve policing problems of mutual concern. Since police protection is a necessity one hundred percent of the time, there are better shifts to work than there are others. Officers will work in and outdoors, in all kinds of weather, and may be required to stand or walk for hours at a time. They may even have to ride in their care for an entire shift. At times, they have to use force and may have to be required to lift twenty-five kilograms in an emergency situation.

A police officer is usually under constant strain, normally working in dangerous situations (normally life threatening). They deal with domestic and public disputes, arresting lawbreakers or pursuing speeding motorists. To fill such a position you need some good personal characteristics. It would include honesty, integrity, good judgement, patience, intelligence, good observation skills and basic good humour that are essential in this occupation.

47. BEST SCHOOLING TIME

Many teenage high school students are tired during the school day, distracting them from their studies. That is just one of the many good reasons that the starting time of school should be later in the day. Some people may say that the brain not being fully functional until 9:30 is just a matter of opinion. Studies have suggested that the average adolescent brain doesn't even start to fully function until around 9:30 am. Many schools already use the suggested later arrival time, so their students can be ready to learn when they arrive at school.

Another thing that everyone knows or remembers about high school is all of the homework that needs to be done for tomorrow. Plus projects that are due, persuasive essays that need to be written, and the time you need to be a teenager. Most students generally have so much work that they'll stay up all night just to get it done. When needing a minimum of 9 hours of sleep as a teenager, getting up at 6:30 to be ready for school is just not enough time. It's easy to think that students will just procrastinate even more, but the average teenager is smarter than you may think.

It sounds absurd to think that students sleep during the school timings. The fact is that many students fall asleep during class. Remember that sleep isn't something that appears according to your opinion. Throwing water on your face, listening to loud music, or taking a shower cannot make your bodies craving for sleep to disappear. The fact is, puberty demands more sleep.

There are also many risks involved with not having proper or adequate amount of sleep. Most people will be very sleepy and drowsy during the day, will have mood and behavioural problems, and even increased vulnerability to drugs and alcohol. These things could also develop more into serious sleeping disorders. Experts advise not to read or watch television shows while unwinding from a day at school or work. Some experts believe that students don't need any more sleep than adults do, but still recommend that the school start time should be later in the daytime. The average high school student just needs a little slack every once in a while they need a way to cope with being a teen. The average teenager needs more sleep.

48. PURPOSE OF EDUCATION

The purpose of our modern education is very delightful. The delicate tools necessary for our intellectual workshop are achieved by schooling. I suspect that our best tools are realized rather automatically, but if there is to be outside influence, then, best it is done early, as the human mind matures all too rapidly. Children are not consumed with anxiety to learn anything; least of all has it ever crossed their minds that they must learn English.

How shall we teach it to them, when the few of us who have begun to know what it is known to be a issue of accommodations, a thing with which order, method, and all that the developing mind first apprehends and rests upon have nothing to do with a single word. A kind of miraculous flowering of man's still unconscious wisdom, preserved to us as a compensation for our many blunderings, as a reward for our patience in confusion and our fundamental faith in life. Education might be defined as a social process by which, skills and beliefs, attitudes and ideas of the previous generations are passed to the new generation; it is a process, which is necessary for the maintenance, achievement and development of man in society.

Gerstner states, "In the public schools we have clung tenaciously to the ideas and techniques of earlier decades and even previous centuries," proving that each generation depends on the preceding generation. This definition assumes a biological view of society, one that grows and evolves with each new generation depending on the growth of previous generations.

49. HIGH SCHOOL VS. COLLEGE

High school and college are very dissimilar. There are the main differences and then there are differences that aren't very distinct. These differences include homework, teacher-student relationships, and attendance policies. In this paper I will discuss the major and minor differences between high school and college. I will also explain why responsibility is a very important factor in high school and college.

In high school most teachers will let you turn in your homework late if you give them an excuse such as, "I forgot it at home" or "It's in my locker." In college if you give your professor one of these excuses they will say, "Too bad." There are also a lot more tests in high school. Usually, there is a test every week or two. Although there are more tests, the work is not as hard. Most of the time you will read aloud in class or go over every point of the homework so that there is no question of what you have to do.

Teachers in college for the most part don't really care whether you are attending the class or not. All it means is that if you are not there, you are going to get a failing grade if it happens too often. Missing too many classes will cause the teacher to withdraw you from the class, resulting in a failing grade. If you do it the smart way you would withdraw from the class yourself because then it would have no negative effect on your overall grade. In high school the teachers are always on you about attendance. If you miss too many days you can fail.

If you are not in class they want to know the reason behind. They also want a note from your parents excusing you from class. Some schools even want your parents to call you in sick if you are not going to be there. If you do not have a note they can write you up for an unauthorized absence and, give you a detention. In college you have greater responsibility. You are an adult, and they expect you to act like one. The teachers expect you to except the consequences if you do not do the required work. In high school the teacher would probably call your parents, and let them know that you aren't doing what you are supposed to do. In college you have to be responsible to succeed. It's all up to you.

The main difference between high school and college is the responsibility factor.

50. THE NEED FOR HONESTY

Everyone heard the tale of the Boy who cried Wolf, right? Sure, shepherd boy thinks he's funny, makes a fuss about imaginary wolfs, villagers come running and find no wolf. Then when wolfs actually do come, he yells and screams, yet villagers weren't about to play his game again, his sheep get nailed by the wolfs. Moral of the story: liars are not believed even when they tell the truth.

The reasons people are less than truthful are many, they do it because they lack the courage to say what they think, they do it because they are comfortable in their pretensions, and they do it because they are insecure. I spent a long time asking myself why should people be straight up, what moral chains are there? It's too easy to say because society expects it, or because history has presented its heroes as paragons of virtue. No, I believe the reason to be much more selfish, the need for people to be straight-up is that individually you become better people for it. But why? Why would you be a better person for speaking the truth? Who knows exactly? All I know is that I hold it high, and I refuse to abnegate this belief for anyone, better yet I expect people to follow suit.

51. FEAR: A GOOD OR BAD THING?

A whole new environment was thrown at the young boy all of a sudden. He had never seen such different people, or so many people altogether. He had reached high school. Before this, he had gone to a small public school, which only consisted of about the number of people in one class in high school, and some classes even surpassed the amount in the entire school. He wasn't sure what to do, where to go; his mind was in a state of blankness. His palms were sweating, along with the rest of his body because of all the beautiful girls he had never seen before; in addition, to make all these matters worse he was a shy guy.

This quiet young man decided to face the facts; he was going to be attending this school for four years, so he might as well make the best of the time being. He didn't know where to start making a good impression, so he started in the classroom. He was intimidated because he had heard the classes were much more arduous compared to the ones in elementary and middle school, but he finally gave it a shot.

According to Webster's New World Dictionary,

"Fear is the anxiety caused by real or possible danger, pain, and fright." There is a gargantuan amount of people who would like to avoid fear altogether, but it is a part of life and without it, life would be extremely boring. The fear people endure can be perceived positively because it can help people do things they never thought of doing; on the other hand, it can deter them from achieving the goals they have set for themselves.

This notion is shown in the following pieces of work: *The Great Gatsby* by F. Scott Fitzgerald, The *Tragedy of Macbeth* by William Shakespeare, and *Cry, the Beloved Country* by Alan Paton. Since the beginning of time, fear has been accompanying everybody that has walked on this planet and may be even on other ones. As H.P. Lovecraft puts it, "The oldest and strongest emotion of mankind is fear". This quote reveals how everything people do is based on how strong the fear in somebody actually is; this determines if they are able to go out and achieve their goal, or just pay attention to the fear and "chicken out". Fear can and should be conquered because it is the only thing hampering anybody from doing what he or she wants. Without fear, people would be able to do anything they want, which would allow people to achieve their goals.

52. THE AIR CRASH

It was early in the morning, warm and sunny. We had the day off from school for some reason, but I can't remember why. I was riding my bike in the street with my friends. Mohan, about four blocks from my home when I heard a faint blast, looked up and saw a jetliner falling out of the sky on fire. I can't remember thinking anything except it's going to hit my house. Then I realized there were probably a lot of people on the plane, and was immediately so scared that I began to cry.

Then I didn't hear anything until the plane hit the ground. Watching that plane on impact is a sensation I hope I never have to relive again. The aircraft was diving at a steep angle and one wing was on fire, with flames shooting everywhere. I remember the plane disappearing behind some tall trees and then feeling the ground shake like an earthquake, and the deafening roar of the impact and following explosion.

It was an absolute nightmare. It seemed like the entire neighbourhood was on fire. The TV stations and news reporters were converging on the scene in what seemed like only a matter of minutes, but must've been at least half an hour. I think I just stood there talking to people for the longest time, but I don't remember anything they said. There were only distant sirens.

In a short period of time the police and several residents had blocked off the streets to traffic, and I remember hearing people screaming in the background, and others yelling for help. I also remember the trees being on fire and this incredible column of black smoke rising into the clear air, and the smell of jet fuel burning. All these people – some firefighters, some police officers, and some ordinary people – were carrying injured people and passengers into the private school across the street. I didn't know then, but some of them were dead. I remember how weird it was that the freeway traffic was completely stopped on I-805, which was only a block from the impact site, and it was eerily quiet except for the distant chaos.

53. MY WRITING - ONE DAY

The one day of my summer vacation that I would love to relive would be this wonderful invigorating night. It all started out as I was sitting on a grassy knoll, I could tell that it was spring time from the cool breeze that was blowing through my hair, and the smell of fresh flowers all around me. The clouds were of pastel colours, and it looked as if an artist had taken a paint brush to a canvas and made a beautiful masterpiece. At the sunset the colours faded, and the night sky looked the deepest blue that my eyes have ever seen. The stars were dancing across the sky, and the man on the moon had an angelic grin as if the stars were there for his entertainment. I looked around and it seemed as if this perfect world of wonderful aromas and glorious sites never ended. I knew I had to go, but I would return there some day.

Then as I opened my eyes, I realized that my day-dream was nothing but a fantasy. Even though in my dreams I still have the vision of this place... this place which I am still in search of...in reality.

54. THE IMPACT OF MUSIC ON MY LIFE

Everyday, I reserve time to collect my thoughts in a journal. This form of writing helps me to understand myself, make wiser choices, and in a sense, keep myself 'in check'. Since I began, I found that the facet in my life that keeps me focused is playing music. Becoming an instrumentalist has been a driving force in my life. Playing has, in many ways, kept me sane. It taught me to harness the talents I possess and apply them in a manner that best suits me. I can truly say that my life would not be the same without the presence of music. If not for playing, I would have never met my best friend, who has seen me through every hardship.

My encounters with Rahul, my high school band director, would have never been, and it is because of him that I have become a sculpted musician. Playing music involves every sense of yourself and displays every emotion through sound.

55. MY TRIP

While vacationing in China last summer I had the opportunity to visit "The Great Wall of China". Combined with its technological feat and awesome presence the "Great Wall of China" could easily be one of man's most remarkable accomplishments. With its design and texture that stretch for miles, it can be an overwhelming experience.

Construction of the Great Wall started in the seventh century B.C; it joined the walls to hold off the invaders from the Xiongnu tribes in the north and extended them to more than 10,000 or 5,000 kilometers. Evenafewmilesawayfrom theGreatWall itsself, you could already see the outline of the wall stretching for miles. Standing near the Great Wall, I notice the cold stale air. It was hard to breathe and I had to constantly cough to keep my throat clear.

Visiting this huge wall of blocks in the morning can be an unforgettable experience. The ground was muddy because it rained non-stop the previous day. Climbing up the stairways that leads up the "Great Wall", I could hear all different languages spoken by the people who were in attendance. On top looking down sideways the wall seems to never end. As far as my eyes could see the road seemed to travel forever.

The weird intertwining design was a unique concept. Touching my hand against the hard brick wall, the texture of the brick was something I never felt before. The style in which the ancient Chinese constructed brick, it withstood the age of time and also forcing enemies from the north. While still pressing my hand against the brick I notice how cold and freezing was the brick. You could place your hand on the same place, but if too long, your hand would start to freeze up. Bricks that were used to create the sidewalls were different than the ones made for the walkway. Every half-mile stood a tower post where the ancient Chinese warriors would look out for attacks. There are no windows, and for emergencies there are rope ladders that can be tossed over the wall for escaping or warning the city of attack.

56. MUSIC IN EDUCATION

Music in education is essential to our children because it increases their listening skills and is a common method of communication for cultures worldwide. There are schools attempting to eliminate teaching musical arts to our children. The board of education claims they must provide education by concentrating on the basic academic courses, but what they don't realize is that music is a major part of basic education. We must not allow them to pull the teaching of music out of our school curriculums because music is an essential form of communication.

Our children do not have to be fluent in the arts to receive the value of broad exposure to the different musical dialogues. Deprivation of a very valuable part of education occurs if we do not teach them to appreciate a wide variety of music. Metaphorically speaking, we often associate the terms 'language' and 'grammar' with the term 'music'. This association leads us to believe that music is a form of language, possibly because no symbol system other than language has the same potential as music of infinite productivity and precision. It takes a multitude of directions and phonetic-type symbolism to produce a pleasant sounding musical composition.

This relates very closely to the requirements of everyday language. The primary objective of any spoken language is to convey a person's thoughts in a comprehensible fashion, but we must remember that everyone thinks and comprehends everything in a different way. Musical language contains vast quantities of words to help people understand how original composers intended to play a specific piece. Musical language also has directions that allow and encourage some scope of original interpretation and minor departures from the written score, resulting in no two performances sounding exactly alike.

57. MY BIRTHDAY

I consider myself blessed in the family department. I have a husband and we have three boys and one girl. We love our children very much and are very determined to give them the best upbringing and lots of wonderful memories. My husband and I agree that making each of our children feel special at least once a day is important, and especially on their birthdays. What I mean by saying, making them feel special everyday, is the comments like "wow you sure are doing a good job" or simply telling them how much you missed them while they were gone to school during the day. Now birthdays are a very big deal; this day is about celebrating life and how thankful your family and friends are that they have you. With all that being said ... our birthday situation is a little more unique than most.

First I'll start by letting you know about the boys, Daya our oldest son, born on September seventh, 1995. Five years and three hundred and fifty nine days later, along came Chaman, bright and early on September first, 2001. Then our third boy Gambhir, born on September ninth, 2004. Now it makes perfect sense to have all three birthday parties on one day, right? Here comes the tricky part, having one party and making sure each of the boy feels comfortable. Let me explain how we have mastered this, and kept the importance of each of their birthdays in mind.

First, each of the boys gets to invite the friends they chose for the party. The party always takes place in our backyard, chosen by the birthday boys of course.

The boys have happily agreed to this problem, agreeing on this because they realize no other location there would be a limit on how many guests they could invite. They enjoy inviting as many people as they want, I think it makes them feel very special to do so. September is a great month for an outside party so we have never had an issue to deal with not having enough space for celebrations.

58. OUR NATIONAL FLAG

India's flag was adopted on July 22, 1947, after she became independent from Great Britain. The flag was based upon the design of the flag of the Indian National Congress.

The Indian flag has three equal horizontal bars (saffron, white and green) with a blue Dharma Chakra (the wheel of law) in the centre. The wheel has 24 spokes, representing the 24 hours in a day (at the end of each spoke is a dark blue half-moon).

The orange (deep saffron) symbolizes courage and sacrifice (saffron is the sacred colour of Hinduism). The white stands for peace, unity and truth. The green stands for fertility (although it originally symbolized Islam). The blue symbolizes the sky and the ocean. The height of this flag is two-thirds of the width.

A National Flag is the most solemn symbol of a country. Even a Head of the State, the King or President, salutes it respectively. A piece of cloth called the National Flag stands for the whole nation, its honour and glory. When it goes up the flag mast, the heart of a true citizen is filled with pride.

Our Tiranga is now over sixty years old, but it is surprising that not a single work exists on it; which gives a history of its development. Whatever information is available on the subject is found in bits and pieces and at times it is incorrect.

A flag is a necessity for all nations. Millions have died for it. It is no doubt a kind of idolatry which it would be a sin to destroy. A flag represents an ideal for its nation. The unfurling of the Union Jack in the English breast evokes sentiments whose strength it is difficult to measure. The Stars and Stripes mean a world to the Americans. The Star and the Crescent will call forth the best bravery in Islam.

It will be necessary for us Indians–Hindus, Muslims, Christians, Jews, Parsis and all other to whom India is their home–to recognize a common flag to live and to die for.

59. MY MOTHER

My mother was born on the third of March, 1951, in a small subarb of Delhi. My mother's childhood was gracious, but not so easy because she was born after the World War II (1941-1945). She was the youngest child in her family. She has one brother and a sister. Her mother was an educated woman, but she did not work because she had to take care of her large family. My mother lived in a private house. Her family had a small garden and domestic animals. When my mother was seven years old, she went to school. Also she attended a music school and can play piano also, my mother was a weak child and was often sick. She decided to go to sports and try to be healthy. After finishing school, my mother entered the university and after five years she became an engineer.

My mother liked to travel and has visited many interesting places. My mother is more like a friend to me. I can talk to her about everything without feeling embarrassed and shy. She even knows all about my friends with whom I meet.

My mother is a very good example for me. The

person who teaches me the most is my mother. She is very responsible and honest. She always teaches me to tell the truth. She is also a very good housewife. Our house is always clean and food is always ready. My mother is a very good cook. She teaches me how to cook and be a good wife for my future husband. My mother likes to read and gives me the same habits. We like to discuss books and articles that we read. As a greedy reader, she gave me the example I imitate to this day. Then, I could not understand how she could stand reading so much nonfiction; I preferred novels. Now I see that her reading provided the necessary tonic to life.

I love my mother very much and she is the best person in my life. So, while I have been profoundly shared by many teachers, the one who taught me how to learn is the one I still call Mom.

60. MY FATHER

My father is a man with a great personality and great thoughts who taught me discipline and importance of life. He is the best father one can ever have. He is six feet tall and has a mustache. You can see how handsome he would be. Since he is a gentleman, he never even thinks towards that direction. My mom is very proud to have him as her husband. He made a lot of sacrifices for his family, turning down many pretty women would be considered as a big sacrifice. He did a lot for his family to give them the best education and the living standard. He sent his brothers abroad for higher education. He continued to sacrifice for us as well. He was and still is a very loving and caring father. My mom tells me, he was there for me everyday, played with me when I was little and even now he gives me time and attention. He really emphasized on education from the very beginning. He gave me the freedom to choose any field that I wanted to succeed in.

In case I would have any kind of a problem, I very well knew where to turn for help. Whether I needed an advice to make a decision or financial help, he was always there for me and thank God he still is there for me.

I remember at one time I was really confused in choosing the company to join. I had two offers and one of them offered a better deal than the other. Since I always seek advise from my father, he advised to join the company which I had thought was not giving me a better deal. The experience that he possessed assured me to take his advise. I am very glad I did that because the other company is out of business right now. My father is a very influential person as well. He helps people in any way he can. No matter how you look at him he is the greatest father one can have. Not only the greatest father, the greatest friend, the greatest husband, etc. May God bless my father and I hope and pray that he stays around for many more years to come!

61. GOOD FRIDAY

Good Friday is the day on which Jesus Christ was crucified. Jesus Christ was born to Marry in Nezareth – a small town in Israel. He was the founder of Christianity, one of the world's largest religions. Christ is believed to be an incarnation of God and his teachings are described in the New Testament.

It is believed that on Good Friday Christ was arrested by clergymen. Hence, Good Friday is believed to be the time when Christians keep fast and celebrate the day over the birth of Christ. Some people believe that 'Good' in GOOD FRIDAY is referred to as 'GOD' and it is also a common belief that 'GOOD' is referred to the gift brought by martyrdom. And according to one of the views, on this day, it is Jesus who went to heaven. It is also celebrated as a festival of life and spirit. Some believe that the word "Good" evolved from "God" or "God's Friday".

He is also considered to be the Son of God – as it is believed that he had certain kind of spark or glow on his face at the time of his birth.

The Good Friday celebration starts by kissing a plank of wood depicted on the cross of Christ. Afte this ritual people perform the other practice which starts from 3 o'clock where narratives are read out from the four gospels of the holy book, and latter on general communion service is performed at midnight, after which a burial takes place. On Good Friday particularly, the bells of the church remain silent (which on other days doesn't) because this day is marked as a SAD DAY for Christians.

People follow the example of Jesus Christ and keep fast on this day as, according to one story, Christ fasted in the desert to overcome the Evil One for forty days before the beginning of his valuable teachings. However, this period of forty days is popularly known as 'Ash Wednesday'. This ends on Lent, also known as 'Good Friday' following the other day, i.e., Easter Sunday. Many people even today perform a three-hour service on Friday in remembrance of the death of Christ in which one service includes seven distinct elements, stating seven utterances of Christ when he was hanged on cross. This incident is famously depicted in the small town near Goa (in India) called Panjim which celebrates Good Friday with a large spirit. Many people gather there to take part in the celebrations which is held in full bloom in the churches.

62. BASKETBALL

As a kid, I always admired basketball as my favaourite game. I always looked forward to see the crowd behind my team and wanted to grow up to be a superstar in basketball. I had not discovered the Lord,s intent about the situation until sometime in high school.

God didn't want me to play basketball and I asked him shortly after the tragedy, O ! Lord, is it only now you tell me this? I learnt how to play organized basketball at the age of twelve and from then on, I had just worked on my speed, agility and endurance in the game. In my first year of high school, I anticipated the game very much. I remember coming out with the team on several occasions to practise, and it was almost the best way to flaunt my skill. It was not long afterwards that I started off practising with the team that I met my fate.

Never had I guessed that I would be laid on the sick bed as a result. We had a game on that day, and the team came out to practise as usual. Almost like a freshman, I was just trying to make my dominance felt on the team, just like any singer would do on concert auditions.

I got jabbed in the belly while in mid-air by one of my teammates and it was the jab I would not forget. I was conscious all the while, with my stomach split inside my tummy. You can imagine the pain of that. I was immediately attended to, but my case needed a first class surgery. I would not want to burrow too deep into the past, but this event would prove to have changed my life forever.

63. FOOTBALL

One week after we went out for summer last year we started preparing ourselves physically for the upcoming season. As a team through the whole summer we lifted and ran four days a week.

That summer was when I knew varsity football was going to be a commitment. The night before we were going to begin double days, two practices every day for a week, we all slept in the gym as one group united as a team. During that evening we discussed and set goals that we would strive for and that would guide our season on a prosperous path.

In order .to maintain at the top we had to go undefeated. This was once again not easy because the season was mostly filled with tough opponents who would not simply allow us to win. I did not play the star role in these games but I was simply on two special teams, kick off and kick return, and played a little time at linebacker. We defeated our first nine opponents and ended up in the playoffs. We gave it our all and won two playoff games versus two of the most competitive opponents I have ever played.

In the championship game the special teams I was on were unbelievable. The kickoff team caused the other team to turnover the ball and the return team returned the ball all the way for a touchdown, the first time all season. I was part of both of these teams and am proud to say it. It was a game that brought me pride and happiness. I can now say that this season was well worth the commitment because the reward was so magnificent.

We were not simply a championship team but a family. Throughout the season we bonded each other and moved each week toward a common goal. It felt so good inside that we fulfilled our goals. I now look at the plaque on my wall and the championship football ring on my hand and words such as: pride, courage, commitment, sacrifice, and family come to mind.

64. STUDENTS AND ATHLETICS

Students should be encouraged to play sports whether for school or just in their spare time, but I recommend it more for a team. This gives them so much and the lessons learned are unforgettable. It teaches teamwork, hard work, dedication, health concern, responsibility, good sportsmanship and so much more. They get confidence and are much better students in general. Players must keep their grades up and are much less likely to do drugs as proven by numerous studies. Even in the off season, they realize how bad health practices can affect their performance. It gives them something to do and keeps them out of trouble. I think athletes are more well rounded people. The only exceptions are the images of other athletes on TV such as Dennis Rodman, that some let the time spent at practice prevent them from doing their full potential in school, injuries, and doing their homework.

Teach them all the strong points that sports can benefit them and watch them strive! It can improve their and other's lives by making them healthier hardworking, and determined. There are so many benefits if the sport is taken seriously. So let them play sports or begin to play one yourself and become a stronger person. All of this from playing a game of fun and challenge!

65. DOLPHINS

Dolphins are mammals closely related to whales and porpoises. Dolphins have a powerful and streamlined body. They are found in all seas and oceans. Dolphins can be told apart from porpoises by their nose, which is beaklike, and also their conical teeth. Porpoises have a flatter nose, sharper teeth, and a more solid body.

There are 32 known species of dolphins. The bottle-nosed dolphin is often the species used in aquatic shows. The common dolphin inspired much Mediterranean folklore. Both of the dolphins above appear in open waters, usually around cruise ships. They like to show off around the boat. There are also freshwater dolphins that live in rivers of Asia and South America. The Buffeo dolphin has been spotted up to 1250 miles up the Amazon River. The buffeo is the smallest of all dolphins averaging about four feet. The bottlenose is closer to ten feet. The killer whale, which is also considered as a dolphin, can grow to 30 feet long. The pilot whale is also considered as a dolphin. Dolphins were once hunted by commercial boats for the small amount of oil that can be extracted from their body. This oil is used to lubricate small parts in watches. Cheaper oils have now been found, so dolphins are not hunted for this reason any more.

Dolphins can be caught in tuna nets by accident. Since dolphins have to breath at the surface they drown in tuna nets. It is estimated that 4.8 million dolphins were killed in tuna nets in 12 years. Under pressure from animal rights activists tuna consumers will not accept tuna from canners that do not protect dolphins. Animal rights activists also believe that dolphins shouldn't be in captivity for use in aquatic shows. Dolphins eat a lot of food in a day, usually about one third of their body weight. A dolphin's diet consists of mostly fish and squid. Dolphins can swim very fast, so they are able to easily catch their food.

66. CAT VS. DOG

Dogs and cats are very different animals and have different attitudes, needs, and habits. Understanding these differences can help in the process of choosing between them. For unwavering love and loyalty, a dog is the better choice. Dogs will not question authority, and they will, after some training, do exactly what they are told to do. There are many species of dogs, and they come in large, medium, and small sizes.

Dogs require a lot of attention, and they will make sure their owners are aware of it. They need to be watched constantly and must be taken regularly for walks, because, as most owners know, a dog cannot be trained to do his business in a litter box. A dog will, however, respond instantly to his owner's every wish and will lie at or on that owner's feet anytime, anywhere.

A dog is very much like a child but it cannot be left alone in the house for too long. It will get bored easily and can, without too much effort, make your house look as if a tornado were just there. On the other hand, for ease of care, or peace and quiet, cats can be a better choice, will only sleep on the bed if they want to, and will sleep at whichever end they choose.

Cats are quite independent, and they do not require much attention, the purring sound a cat makes is one of the few indications of its love. They will only make a mess of the house if they are upset or sick. Cats and dogs are wonderful pets, and they both give many years of companionship. They are soothing to the soul, and they teach responsibility.

The decision regarding which to choose, then, is one of duty. The pet-owner must decide how much effort he or she wants to put forth. If a loyal, loving pet and trustworthy companion is desired, the dog is a good choice. If, conversely, quiet and low maintenance is more important, a cat is a better choice.

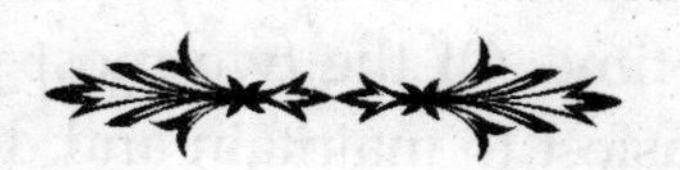

67. CATS

Many people today have pets for pleasure and companionship. Nearly any animal can be a pet, such as hamsters, rabbits, birds, fish, frogs, horses, and even cats and dogs. Besides being a loving companion, pets serve many other purposes, as in protecting homes, destroying vermin, and providing a means of transportation.

The elderly and the childless couples can rely on a pet as an emotional outlet. In addition, pets can be kept for their beauty, rarity, or for the beautiful sounds that birds can make. Today pets are usually purchased from breeders, pet shops, or animal shelters rather than individually captured and tamed. All pets were made domestic, including cats.

Cats are the second most popular pets in the world at this time. Of the two most popular pets, cats are the easiest to maintain and do not need to be taken out for exercise. Being small means cats are not big eaters and only have to eat one or two times a day. Cats can play with string, balls, and anything that may fascinate them.

On the other hand, cats can be your companion while you sleep, read a book, or watch television. The life of a cat can be very interesting if you are willing to spend time with them and learn their personality. Every cat has its own personality. Cats can live to be 15 years old, and in that time a cat-owner can find that the cat is a man's best friend. The origins of cat can be very interesting, considering that the cat first began its life with the early Egyptians and other cultures.

68. WHALES

The blue whale is the largest creature of the sea; in fact, it's the largest creature known to man. Contrary to what most people think, even though blue whales live in the sea, they are mammals.

They breathe air, have their babies born alive, and can live anywhere from 30 to 70 years. The blue whale is a baleen whale, and instead of having teeth, blue whales have around 300-400 baleen plates in their mouths. Baleen is rows of coarse, bristle-like fibres used to strain plankton from the water. Baleen is made of keratin, the same material as our fingernails.

The pleated throat grooves allow the blue whale's throat to expand during the huge intake of water during filter feeding; they can "hold 1,000 tons or more of food and water when fully expanded."

The average may be about 50-70 throat grooves. Blue whales grow up to about 80 feet (25 m) long on an average, weighing about 120 tons. The females are generally larger than the males, this is the case for all baleen whales. "The largest specimen found was a female 94 feet (29 m) long weighing more than

174 tons." The head of the Blue whale forms up to a quarter of the total body length. Compared with other rorquals, the head is very broad. The blue whale's heart is also large, the size of a small car and can pump almost ten tons of blood throughout the body. They also have a very small, falcate (sickle-shaped) dorsal fin that is located near the fluke, or tail. Blue whales have long, thin flippers eight feet (2.4 m) long and flukes that are 25 feet (7.6m) wide. The blue whale's skin is usually blue-gray with white-gray spots.

69. ANIMAL-TESTING

Every year, millions of animals undergo painful suffering or death as a result of scientific research into the effects of drugs, food additives, cosmetics and other chemical products.

While most people think animal-testing is necessary, others are upset by what they see as needless suffering. This essay looks at some of the positive and negative aspects of animal-testing.

Many medical treatments and procedures have been developed from experiments on animals. Since animals share many features with humans, scientists use animals to test the safety and effectiveness of newly developed drugs before pilot-testing on small groups of patients. Medical teams practise new operating techniques such as transplants on animals. Without animal-testing, many procedures or new drugs would be extremely unsafe.

However, many people are concerned that animals are suffering unnecessarily and cruelly. They do not believe that every new drug needs to be tested on animals, especially with the huge database of knowledge and modern computer models.

They also are worried that many animal tests are ineffective, pointing out that many drugs have had to be withdrawn from the market despite extensive testing. They particularly feel that animal-testing should not be used for non-essential products such as cosmetics, shampoos, soaps, and cleaning products. Furthermore, some campaigners would like to see certain tests replaced and more humane methods used.

We need to make sure that the millions of animals who are used for testing new products are treated with the minimum of suffering. Although some animal-testing may be unavoidable at present, treating our fellow creatures as mercifully as possible will demonstrate our humanity.

70. THE BEE

The worker bees live a very short life. Their average life span is about six weeks. The worker bees are the sterile females of the bee population. They feed honey and pollen to the queen of the hive. The worker bees are called nurse bees when they enter into this stage. They produce a jelly called royal jelly which is high in protein. They give this royal jelly to the queen bee and she feeds it to her young ones. Then worker bees start to produce a honeycomb from the wax that they secrete. During this stage they can also fan their wings to circulate fresh air.

The house bee is a young worker bee about two weeks old who only works in the hive. The queen bee is the head honcho of the whole hive. The queen really doesn't do much. She sits in the hive and has the babies. The queen secretes a substance called 'queen factor' which keeps all of the other female bees from becoming sexually mature. The queen is fed royal jelly to further her development as she becomes a grown bee. The queen's number one priority is to reproduce. Once she successfully does that, her job is pretty much done with.

The queen is very special because she can do all of her mating in the air. The queen only mates once in her life, but in that one mating session she can produce as many as a million eggs a year. When the queen feels that the hive is getting crowded, she ventures off into the wilderness with a few of her worker bees to search for a new beginning (a new hive). Then, when the queen dies another queen will take her place and start the whole thing all over again.

The drones are also placed on this earth for one main reason. That reason is to satisfy the queen. Drones are unfertilized eggs whose jobs consist of supplying the queen bee with the sperm when she is ready. Then the drones are either eaten by the queen or stung by the workers and evicted from their home. They live a very tragic life. The drone's structure is also kind of odd because the drone does not possess a stinger. So, they cannot really protect themselves when they need to. The queen bee releases the substance called queen factor which is a pheromone.

71. DIFFERENT ANIMALS

In the beginning before the great storm, lived a follower of God named Noah. The Earth had only one continent with many beautiful animals. Noah the watcher of these creatures received a message from God. One night, Noah prayed to God for an answer of why the animals seemed uneasy lately and how to solve it; God then let him on the secret of the great storm to come. God then told Noah to take two of every animal and put him or her on a boat, so they can survive the storm.

Noah having faith in God did exactly what God asked him to do and built the boat. He then took two of every animal and put him or her on this great boat called the Arc. Later that day like God said, the great storm swept the land for months. The entire earth at one moment seemed to be a great sea. Once the storm stopped the water level returned and Noah hit the first piece of land. He then let the animals run free and wild in this new tropic environment. The animals immediately started to reproduce and had many babies.

Soon the animal population got too massive for the small island and Noah found many animals not getting along with one another. So he then looked to God's aid once again. God answered, and told him that, "Now the storm is over, Noah, you must return some of the animals to different parts of this world." Since the island could not supply enough food and space for all these creatures, God said to follow a special bird of different colours and to drop different animals in other islands of the world. He did so and took six groups of each animal and pair by pair put them in different parts of the world. Some in cold arctic areas while others in hot dessert areas. Noah prayed for their safe passage and wished them luck in their newfound home. God looked after each animal and saw to it that they were able to exist in their new environment.

72. DIWALI

Diwali is one of the most important festival, hugely waited and immensely cherished festival celebrated across India. Diwali celebrations spread across five days, with each day having its own significance and set of rituals.

The first day is called "Dhanteras", on which new utensils and silver ware is brought to the house. The second day is called "Choti Diwali", which normally involves preparation for the next day and the tradition of playing cards is observed in many families.

The next day, or third day is the "Badi Diwali", which involves the worshipping of mother Lakshmi. The fourth day is the Govardhan Puja and finally the five days end with Bhai Dooj.

The festival of Diwali is truly a "Festival of Lights", as it not only involves lighting of lamps but it brings the light of happiness, togetherness, spiritual enlightens and prosperity for everyone.

With the sounds of crackers killing all bad omens, the lighted lamps lighting the lives of people, the prayers and pujas creating an atmosphere full of goodness and purity, the festival of Diwali indeed fills the atmosphere with an aura of goodness and heaven-like atmosphere.

According to the Hindu calendar, the festival of Diwali is celebrated on the new moon day that marks the end of Ashwin and beginning of Kartik month. In 2010, it will fall on 5th November.

73. DUSSEHRA

In the months of Ashwin and Kartik, the Hindus observe a 10-day ceremony of fast, rituals, celebrations, fiests to honour the mother Goddess and the triumph of Lord Rama over the demon Ravana. Dussehra also symbolizes the triumph of warrior Goddess Durga over the buffalo demon Mahishasura. Thus, it is a celebration of victory of good over evil.

This celebration starts from Navratri and ends with the tenth day festival of Dussehra. Navratri and Dussehra is celebrated throughout the country at the same time, with varying rituals, but with great enthusiasm and energy as it marks the end of the scorching summer and the start of winter season.

The tenth day after Navratri is called Dussehra, on which a number of fairs are organized throughout northern India, with burning effigies of Ravana. The Ramlila - an enactment of the life of Lord Rama, is held during the nine days preceding Dussehra. On the tenth day Dussehra or Vijay Dasami, larger than life effigies of Ravana, his son and brother, Meghnadh and Kumbhakarna, are set to fire.

The main importance and significance of the festival of Dussehra is the rise of "good over evil". There are many legends behind the celebration of Dussehra, all depicting that ultimately it's the "good" that wins.

Among the Hindus, Lord Rama is considered to have a culmination of all the best qualities that a human can possess, required to make this world a happy place. Both the festivals of Diwali and Dussehra are celebrated in honour of Lord Rama and his morals. Dussehra is the tenth day of Navratri, while Diwali is celebrated 20 days ahead of Dussehra. Lord Rama emerged victorious in a ferocious battle against Ravana who had abducted Sita. Inspite of all powers that Ravana possessed, it was ultimately the good intensions of Lord Rama that saw the face of victory. This is generally depicted on the day of Dussehra by burning the effigies of Ravana and Lord Rama's bow that kills him. People every year on this day get the moral of leading a righteous life.

74. HOLI

Holi is the festival of colour and is marked as the opening festival in Hindu calendar that falls on the full moon day in the month of Phalgun. People enjoy themselves playing with many colours and celebrate the whole day with much pomp and gaiety.

Originally Holi was regarded to be the festival of celebrating good harvests and fertility of the land. There are several legends and stories behind Holi. A popular legend says that Holi is remembered for the sacrifice of Holika who burnt herself in fire on this day.

Holi is regarded as one of the most ancient festivals of the Aryans who find an honoured mention in our old Sanskrit texts like Dashakumar Charita and Garud Puran. Even the play Ratnavali written by Harshdev states a delightful description of Holi as a festival. In those days this festival was celebrated as Vasantotsav. Latter the festival was renamed as Madanotsav.

Celebrations of Holi festival is characterized by performing Holi puja as per Hindu tradition. Dhulendi, which falls the day after Holi Puja, is considered to be the actual festival of colours. Children and youngsters vie with each other by using fast and sticky colours to celebrate Holi. It is great fun and joy for them.

The spirit of Holi is colour - rich and vibrant, flung into the air and smeared with laughter on friends and loved ones. It recalls, very simply, the secret of life: a shifting panorama of sights, movement and feelings. Colours denote energy, vivid, passion and the pulse of life.

These are dry colours that are sold days before the festival actually begins. Markets are flooded with heaps of gulal - they are arranged in pyramids and sold loose. Vendors sit on street corners selling gulal to passers-by. Gulal is made up of many rich colours like pink, magenta, red , yellow and green. 'Abeer' is made of small crystals or paper like chips of mica. This is usually mixed with the gulal to give it a rich shine. These colours can be used dry, or mixed with water. New brides make silver or gold colour from powders especially available in the market.

75. RAKSHA-BANDHAN

The Rakhi festival or Raksha-bandhan has a special significance in the hearts of brothers and sisters in India. The silken thread of Rakhi symbolizes the love between siblings. The Rakhi festival symbolizes all aspects of protection of the good from evil forces. Rakhi is meant to sweeten the ties of brother and sister. Rakhi is celebrated with great joy and excitement al around India. It is widely known as Raksha-bandhan in other parts of the country. Rakhi festival showcases the love, affection and feeling of brotherhood.

Raksha-bandhan usually falls in late August. The main ritual consists of tying the 'Rakhi' knot on to a brother's wrist. 'Raksha-bandhan' literally mean 'Bond of Protection' and implies that while the siste prays to God for the well-being and prosperity of he brother, the brother vows to protect her against all the evils of the world and help her in all the upcoming problems. The day is all about Raksha or protection The values, emotions and the sentiments attached to the customs of Rakhi festival are worth inculcating by the whole human race, the sentiments of harmony and peaceful co-existence.

Rakhi is celebrated with great excitement and joy across India and other parts of the world where Indians reside. From early morning everybody starts getting ready for the occasion. On the day people generally prefer to wear traditional wears. Men mostly wear kurta-pyjama on this occasion whereas women prefer to wear sari or salwar suits, which are mainly Indian traditional clothes. People generally prefer to wear cotton material cloth, as this is comfortable during this season. But with the changing fashion trends every year, people tend to follow the fashion of that season during the festival time. But for Indians, the traditional and cultural chord is so strong that no matter where the siblings are, they will try to wear traditional Indian clothes that reflect our values, tradition and culture. On the occasion of Rakhi, special dishes are prepared, which includes sweets and namkeens. The day has a deeper perspective in today's scenario.

76. NEW YEAR'S DAY

New Year symbolizes the rejuvenation time that coming year brings with it new dreams to be accomplished, goals to be achieved and wishes to be fulfilled. People around the globe celebrate New Year with lots of joy and excitement all around. Everyone bids farewell to the current passing year and welcomes the arriving New Year. It is an occasion when rejoicing bids farewell to the passing year with a grand welcome to the New Year.

The time and celebration of New Year varies from region to region and religion to religion across the world. This is because people in different parts of the world use different calendars. Some calendars are based on the movement of the moon; others are based on the position of the sun, while others are based on both the sun and the moon. All over the world, there are special beliefs about New Year.

Celebrations for the occasion start from 31st December eve only and blast to the zenith at the stroke of 12 midnight. People enjoy together with family and friends, having great time together in relishing lip-smacking food or dancing to the beats.

The New Year comes with many traditions associated with it. Different regions of the world follow different practices on the day. The most commonly followed practices are adopting New Year's resolution, exchanging gifts, lighting crackers at midnight and of course to wish luck and happiness to everyone by three magical words " HAPPY NEW YEAR!"

77. TEACHERS' DAY

In India 5th September is celebrated as Teachers' day as a mark of tribute to the contribution made by teachers to the society. On 5th september, the great teacher Dr. Sarvapalli Radhakrishnan was born who was a staunch believer in education, and was a well-known diplomat, scholar and President of India.

When Dr. Radhakrishnan became the President of India in 1962, he was approached by some of his students and friends who requested him to allow to celebrate 5th September, his "birthday". In reply, Dr. Radhakrishnan said, "Instead of celebrating my birthday separately it would be my proud privilege if September 5 is celebrated as Teachers' day." The request showed Dr. Radhakrishnan's love for the teaching profession. From then onwards, the day has been observed as Teachers' Day in India.

One of the most celebrated writers in modern India, his work varies on philosophical, theological ethical, educational, social and cultural subjects. He contributed numerous articles to different well-known journals, which are of immense value and seem to surprise various readers because of the depth in the meaning of the articles. Teachers mold the lives that they influence because the lessons learned from teachers remain with their students throughout life.

We should always respect our teachers. Teachers need encouragement and support from the community to feel that their devotion to students is appreciated. Teachers' day is now one of the occasions that is looked forward by the teachers and students alike as on this occasion it's not only when teachers are praised but also around various schools students dress up as a representation of their teachers and take various lectures that are assigned to the teachers they represent. As the day passes the students perform the regular activities that are performed by the teachers. On this day students realize what it means to be a teacher and what it means to control the future of several students in their classes and also teachers are reminded what it felt like when they were the students.

78. REPUBLIC DAY

Republic Day is celebrated on January 26th every year and is one of India's most importan national events. It was on January 26th, 1950 tha the Constitution of India came into force and Indi became a truly sovereign, democratic and republi state.

On this day India finally enjoyed the freedon of spirit, rule of law and fundamental principle o governance. The patriotic fervor of the Indian peopl on this day brings the whole country together eve in her embedded diversity.

Republic Day is celebrated most majesticall in the capital, New Delhi, where symbols of th great nation's military might and cultural wealt are displayed in one of the world's most impressiv parades. All Government buildings are illuminate lending the city the atmosphere of a fairyland. Th day is celebrated with much zeal and pride all acros the country.

India gained independence on August 15, 194 But till January 26, 1950, it did not have the prop law of the land for ruling the country.

On this particular date in 1950 the Constitution of India came into force and India became a true nation state in the true sovereign and republic sense.January 26 was not some random date picked out of the calendar. It was on this date in 1927 that the Indian National Congress, then fighting its non-violent war for freedom, voted for complete independence as against 'dominion status'. It was the date when members of the INC took the pledge to work towards a 'sovereign democratic republic' of India.

79. CHRISTMAS DAY

December 25th is celebrated as the birth anniversary of Lord Jesus Christ, who is believed to be born on the same date at Bethlehem, the land of Jews. The festival is celebrated as a mark of respect to Lord Jesus, who is considered as the son of God and founder of the Christian religion.

Christmas is basically celebrated by the Christians but it is also celebrated by other communities around the world. Our modern Christmas is a product of hundreds of years of both secular and religious traditions from around the world.

Many of the most popular Christmas customs including Christmas trees, mistletoe, Christmas presents, and Santa Claus are modern incarnations of the depraved pagan rituals ever practiced on earth.

'Merry Christmas' is a common phrase exchanged amongst Christians. As defined in the modern day, 'Merry' means cheerful or festive. However, the most widely accepted meaning of the word is peaceful or blessed.

Therefore, wishing someone Merry Christmas is truly wishing him a peaceful or blessed "Mass of Christ".

80. INDEPENDENCE DAY

On 15 August 1947, India attained freedom from the British rule. Every year, August 15 is celebrated as the Independence Day in India. This national festival is celebrated with great enthusiasm all over the country.

The Independence Day of any country is a moment of pride and glory. The Prime Minister's speech at the Red Fort in Delhi is a major highlight. Patriotic presentations by school children add colour to the celebrations.

The Prime Minister sets the mood by hoisting the national flag and addressing the nation from the Red Fort, the historical monument in Delhi. This is accompanied by a march-past of the armed and police forces. Similar ceremonies are held in all the state capitals. The Prime Minister's address and the march-past are relayed live on national television.

On August 15, Independence Day is celebrated in a mood of abandon and joy, no rituals, just festivities. It is also a national holiday, when educational institutions, private and government organisations remain closed for official celebrations in the morning.

Schools and colleges mark the day with cultural activities, drills, flag-hoisting and distribution of sweets. Government as well as private organisations celebrate it similarly.

Families and friends get together for lunch or dinner, or for an outing. Housing colonies, cultural centres, clubs and societies hold entertainment programmes and competitions, usually based on the freedom theme.

81. CHILDREN'S DAY

Children's day is a special day for children. Universally, Children's Day is celebrated on 20th November, every year. But in India it is celebrated on 14th November, because the date marks the birth anniversary of legendary freedom-fighter and independent India's first Prime Minister, Pandit Jawaharlal Nehru.

As a tribute to Nehru and his love for children, Children's Day is celebrated on his date of birth. This day reminds to each and every one of us, to renew our commitment to the welfare of children and teach them to live by their Chacha Nehru's quality and dream.

For the children it is a day of much fun and fanfare. On this day various departments of government announce various schemes and organizes various competitions and events for the children. Most schools and corporate institutions conduct competitions for children. Various competitions like quizzes, fancy dress competitions, and elocutions are organised on this day. Electronic media also air special programmes for children to mark the day.

Children celebrate the day with singing, dancing and storytelling in schools and colleges. For the children it is a day of joy and freedom. On this day parents and teachers send cards to their childrens.

82. GANDHI JAYANTI

Gandhi Jayanti is celebrated on 2nd October every year as the birthday of Mahatma Gandhi, known as Father of Indian Nation. Gandhiji, as he was popularly called, proved that non-violence is the most effective instrument of social change. His teachings are promoted to avoid violence and find peaceful solutions to conflicts.

Through his sheer dedication and self-belief, Gandhi freed India from the British. He proved to the world that freedom can be achieved through the path of non-violence.

For Gandhi 'non-violence' and 'truth' were two inalienable virtues. He summed up the entire philosophy of his life as : "The only virtue I want to claim is truth and non-violence. I lay no claim to super human powers : I want none."

When the nation was rejoicing independence (1947), Gandhi went to Noakhali to ameliorate the conditions of the communal riot victims. On 30th January 1948, Gandhi was assassinated in New Delhi by Nathuram Godse who held him responsible for weakening India by insisting upon a payment to Pakistan.

Mahatma Gandhi was a simple man, with simple tastes and high values. Respecting that, even though Gandhi Jayanti is one of the three official national holidays, the festivities are minimal.

A prayer meeting is held at Rajghat, Gandhi's Samadhi in New Delhi. To mark respect that Gandhi had for all the religions and communities, representatives from different religions take part in it.

Verses and prayers are read out from the holy books of all the religions. Gandhi's favourite song, 'Raghupati Raghava Raja Ram', is invariably sung at all the meetings associated with him. Prayer meetings are held in various state capitals as well.

Gandhi Jayanti is observed all over the country, both in government and non-government forums.

83. RED FORT

The Red Fort is part of the city of Shahjahanabad. Its construction was started in 1638 by Emperor Shahjahan and completed in 1648. It is built of red sandstone and has turrets and bastions. The fort is surrounded by a moat in the northeast corner of the city. The wall is 2 km long and varies in height from 18 m. on the river front to 33 m. in the city.

The fort contains all the important buildings of Mughal government like the Halls of Public and Private Audience, Diwan-I-Aam and Diwan-I-Khas, marble palaces, private apartments, a mosque, and elaborately designed gardens. It was attacked by the Persian emperor Nadir Shah in 1739 and by the British soldiers during the war of independence in 1857.

Entrance to the fort is through the imposing Lahore Gate, which takes its name from the fact that it faces Lahore, now in Pakistan. This gate was built by Aurangzeb during his reign and is also known as the Laj Ki Diwar. There is a story that the bazaar of Chandini Chowk was visible from the Diwan-I-Aam. The nobles had to mount down the horse while crossing the bazaar when the emperor was presiding over the hall. Aurangzeb got the wall constructed to make the nobles free from discomfort.

The other attractions within the Red Fort are the Royal Baths or Hamams, the Shahi Burj, Shahjahan's private working area and the Moti Masjid or the Pearl Mosque, built by Aurangzeb for his personal use. The Rang Mahal or the Palace of Colours was the living chamber of the Emperor's wives and mistresses. This palace was crowned with gilded turrets, delicately painted and decorated with an intricate mosaic of mirrors, and a ceiling overlaid with gold and silver that was reflected in a central pool in the marble floor.

Today, the Red Fort is one of the most popular tourist destinations in Old Delhi, attracting thousands of visitors every day and is an eloquent reminder of the glory of the Mughal era.

84. TAJ MAHAL

Since many years, the Taj Mahal has inspired many people. It was one of the most immaculate architectural creations of the world. It has drawn people from all walks of life to witness this ultimate memorial and few have been unmoved by its unmatched beauty. Taj Mahal was not only the symbol of Shahjahan's love for his wife but also encompassed a design combing different cultures and was built with a sophistication unknown to the period.

Persian for crown and palace, the Taj Mahal was built for the wife of Shahjahan to memoralize her. Shahjahan's wife, Mumtaz Mahal, died after the birth of her 14th child. The Taj Mahal stands in the city of Agra, India, located in the northern state of Uttar Pradesh on the banks of the Yamuna river.

The design of the Taj Mahal is a combination of Islamic, Persian, Hindu and earlier Mughal architecture. Hindu craftsmen, sculptors and stone-cutters were involved in creating the Taj Mahal The Taj Mahal was surrounded by the Charbagh Garden, which was introduced to India by the first

Mughal emperor Babur. Babur had his inspiration for the gardens from the Persians. The garden was designed as a rectangle and destined as a reflection of an ideal garden. The perimeter of the Taj Mahal was surrounded by walls except for the side facing the river. Outside the perimeter of the Taj Mahal there were several other mausoleums and structures. Majority of the exterior structures were built primarily out of red sandstone.

The construction of the Taj Mahal began between 1631 and 1654 by a workforce of 20,000, which were recruited from all across northern India. The land had to be excavated and filled with dirt to reduce seepage from the river before construction began. The entire site was raised 50 m. above the river. The Taj Mahal spanned 180 feet in the sky, with a 60 ft by 50 ft dome.

85. INDIRA GANDHI

Indira Gandhi was born on November 19, 1917 at her grandfather's house in Allahabad, in northern India. She was born to Jawaharlal Nehru and Kamala Kaul. Her political career started at the age of 12. She has been the first female Prime Minister and the third Prime Minister of India Her charm, intelligence and charisma made her a powerful statesperson, much loved and admired by her people.

She was the founder and leader of the Monkey Brigade, which was a group of youngsters whose purpose was to help end British control in India. As the leader she relayed information to the children of the group who then went out and warned the people who were going to be arrested by the British. The Indian National Congress was well aware of the Monkey Brigade, and one of the most important actions of the Monkey Brigade was carried out by Indira herself.

She passed her Matric from Pune University and was then sent on to Shantiniketan, established by Rabindranath Tagore in Calcutta.

She married Feroze Gandhi, in March 1941 much against the wishes of the conservative Hindu community, as he was a Parsee. But Nehru was on her side. When Indira's father was in jail he used to write beautiful, long letters to her about his patriotic feelings and the current political situation. This led her to understand the intricacies of the nation, better than the most. In 1942, she joined the 'Quit India' movement along with her husband and was arrested and jailed.

On 31st October 1984, Indira Gandhi's bodyguards as a revenge of the Golden Temple assault, assassinated the prime minister at her Safdarjung Road residence.

86. JAWAHARLAL NEHRU

Jawaharlal Nehru was born on November 14, 1889 in Allahabad. His father Motilal Nehru was a prominent advocate and early leader of the Indian independence movement. The younger Nehru graduated from Cambridge University, and returned to India in 1912. Over the next thirty years, he rose to become the top political leader of the Indian National Congress and struggled for independence from Britain. He was jailed seven times.

After independence he served as India's first Prime Minister from 1947 until he died in 27th May, 1964. He was a great internationalist, and one of the founders of the non-aligned movement.

Nehru was a renowned orator. He could give many extemporaneous speeches in a single day. His most famous speech was the "Tryst with Destiny" address to the Constituent Assembly of India in New Delhi on the night of August 14th and 15th, 1947.

"Long years ago we made a tryst with destiny, and now the time comes when we shall redeem our pledge, not wholly or in full measure, but very substantially. At the stroke of the midnight hour, when the world sleeps, India will awake to life and freedom. A moment comes, which comes but rarely in history, when we step out from the old to the new, when an age ends, and when the soul of a nation, long suppressed, finds utterance. It is fitting that at this solemn moment we take the pledge of dedication to the service of India and her people and to the still larger cause of humanity."

87. GURU NANAK DEV JI

Guru Nanak Dev the well known as the founder of Sikhism, was born on 15th November, 1469 at Rai-Bhoi-di Talwandi in the present district of Shekhupura, Pakistan. The birthday of Guru Nanak Sahib is celebrated on 15th Kartik Puranmashi full moon day of the month Kartik.

On this day the birthday of Guru Nanak Sahib is celebrated every year. (but some other chronicles state that Guru Nanak was born on 20th October, 1469). Guru Nanak's father, Mehta Kalyan Das, more popularly known as Mehta Kalu was the agent and chief accountant of Rai Bular.

Guru Nanak's mother was Mata Tripta, a simple, pious and extremely religious woman. Nanak had an elder sister, Nanki, who always cherished her younger brother.

God had provided him with a contemplative mind and rational thinking. At the age of seven, he learnt Hindi and Sanskrit. He surprised his teachers with the sublimity of his extraordinary knowledge about divine things. At the age of thirteen, he learned Persian and by the age of 16, he was the most learned young man in the region. He was married to Mata Sulakhniji, who gave birth to two sons: Sri Chand and Lakhmi Das. As a social reformer Guru Nanak Dev upheld the cause of women, downtrodden and the poor. He was a reformer as well as a revolutionary. God had endowed him with a contemplative mind and pious disposition. Guru Arjan Sahib called him "the image of God, may, God Himself."

88. WHO IS JESUS

Hundreds of years before Jesus' birth, the Old Testament of the Bible recorded the words of the prophets of Israel predicting his arrival. The Old Testament, written by many people over a period of 1,500 years, contains more than 300 prophecies describing his appearance. All of these details came true, including his miraculous birth, his sinless life, his many miracles, his death and his resurrection. The life Jesus led, the miracles he did, the words he spoke, his death on the cross, his resurrection, his ascent to heaven all point to the fact that he was not merely man, but more than man.

Jesus claimed, I and the Father are one, He who has seen me has seen the Father, and I am the way, and the truth, and the life; no one comes to the Father except through Me. As we study scripture and the life of Jesus, we realize that his life and message cause change.

Jesus was born in Bethlehem in Judea, in the south of Palestine. He grew up in a very ordinary town, named Nezareth, located in Galilee, which was in the north of Palestine. Jesus was a carpenter, but at the age of 30, He became a religious teacher, moving from town to town. In Luke 4:14-22, we read what happened when Jesus began teaching. He went to the synagogue, which was the local place of worship. Although he probably had no more religious education than the average Jewish man, people wanted to hear him. Wherever his teachings and influence have gone, the holiness has flowed. In my life he has been the biggest influence and the people around me. I have never gone wrong when I have followed his teachings, and I never will as long as I live. He works in big ways and most of the time I don't understand but it is always for the good.

89. MAHATMA GANDHI

Mohandas Karamchand Gandhi was born in Porbandar, India, on October 2, 1869. Although his father was a chief minister for the Maharaja of Porbandar, the family came from the traditional caste of grocers (the name Gandhi means "grocer"). His mother's religion was Jainism, a Hindu religion in which ideas of non-violence and vegetarianism are very important. Gandhi said that he was most influenced by his mother, whose life "was an endless chain of fasts and vows." When, in the company of boyhood friends, he secretly smoked, ate meat, told lies, or wore western clothing, he had an intense feeling of guilt. These feelings forced him to make resolutions about his moral behaviour that were to stay with him for the rest of his life.

Gandhi married at the age of 13 years. When he was 18, he went to London to study law. He was admitted to the bar in 1891 and for a while he was attorney in Bombay.

Albert Einstein said about him: "The coming generations will scarcely not believe that such a man as this ever in flesh and blood walked upon this Earth."

90. RAJIV GANDHI

Rajiv Gandhi was born on August 20, 1944 in Bombay (Mumbai) in India's most famous political family. His grandfather Jawaharlal Nehru played a stellar role in India's freedom struggle and became independent India's first Prime Minister. His parents lived separately and Rajiv Gandhi was raised at his grandfather's home where her mother lived.

Rajiv Gandhi was the youngest Prime Minister of India. He became Prime Minister at the age of 40. Rajiv Gandhi came from a family that had great political lineage. He was the eldest son of Indira and Feroze Gandhi. Her mother Indira Gandhi and grandfather Jawaharlal Nehru were Prime Ministers of India. He made a valuable contribution in modernizing Indian administration.

He won his first Lok Sabha election in 1981 from Amethi , the erstwhile constituency of his brother. Soon he became the General Secretary of the Congress Party. After the assassination of Indira Gandhi in October 1984 he became the Prime Minister of India. He called for general elections in 1984 and riding on a massive sympathy wave led

Congress to a thumping victory. Congress garnered 80 percent of the seats in the lower house and achieved its greatest victory since independence.

His wife, Sonia Gandhi, stood by Rajiv's stand of not entering into politics. But after constant requests from his mother Indira Gandhi, he decided to contest. His entry was criticized by many in the press, public and opposition political parties. They saw the entry of Nehru-Gandhi scion into politics as a forced, hereditary, participation. Within a few months of his election as a Member of Parliament, Rajiv Gandhi acquired significant party influence and became an important political advisor to his mother. He was also elected as the general secretary of the All-India Congress Committee and subsequently became the president of the Youth Congress.

On 21 may 1991, on his way towards the dais, Rajiv Gandhi was garlanded by many of his supporters and well wishers. At around 10 pm, the assassin greeted him and bent down to touch his feet. She then exploded an RDX explosive-laden belt attached to her waist-belt killing him.

91. GAUTAM BUDDHA

Siddhartha Gautama was a spiritual teacher in the northern region of the Indian subcontinent who founded Buddhism. He is generally seen by Buddhists as the Supreme Buddha of our age. His birth and death timings are uncertain. The early 20th-century historians date his lifetime from c. 563 BCE to 483 BCE; more recently, however, at a specialist symposium on this question, the majority of those scholars who presented definite opinions gave dates within 20 years either side of 400 BCE for the Buddha's death, with others supporting earlier or later dates.

Siddhartha, said to have been destined to a luxurious life as a prince, had three palaces (for seasonal occupation) especially built for him. His father, King Śuddhodana, wishing for Siddhartha to be a great king, shielded his son from religious teachings or knowledge of human suffering. Siddhartha was brought up by his mother's younger sister.

As the boy reached the age of 16, his father arranged his marriage to Yaśodharā , a cousin of the same age. According to the traditional account, in time, she gave birth to a son, Rahula. Siddhartha spent 29 years as a Prince in Kapilavastu. Although his father ensured that Siddhartha was provided with everything he could want or need, Siddhartha felt that material wealth was not the ultimate goal of life.

Gautama, also known as Shakyamuni ("Sage of the Shakyas"), is the key figure in Buddhism, and accounts of his life, discourses, and the monastic rules are believed by Buddhists to have been summarized after his death and memorized by his followers. Various collections of teachings attributed to Gautama were passed down by oral tradition, and first committed to writing about 400 years later. Early Western scholarship tended to accept the biography of the Buddha presented in the Buddhist scriptures as largely historical, but currently "scholars are increasingly reluctant to make unqualified claims about the historical facts of the Buddha's life and teachings."

92. ASOKA THE GREAT

Asoka was one of the most powerful kings of the Indian subcontinent. A ruler of the Mauryan Empire, Asoka ruled over the country from 273 BC to 232 BC. The reign of Emperor Asoka covered most of India, South Asia and beyond, stretching from present day Afghanistan and parts of Persia in the west, to Bengal and Assam in the east, and Mysore in the south. However, the Battle of Kalinga changed King Asoka completely. From a power-hungry emperor, he turned into a Buddhist follower and started preaching the principles of Buddhism throughout the world.

Asoka was born in 304 BC, to Mauryan Emperor Bindusara and a relatively lower ranked queen, Dharma. The legend associated with the emperor goes that his birth had been predicted by Buddha, in the story of 'The Gift of Dust'. Buddhist Emperor Asoka had only one younger sibling, Vitthasoka, but, several elder brothers. Right from his childhood days Asoka showed great promise in the field of weaponry skills as well as academics.

Asoka quickly grew into an excellent warrior general and to an astute statesman. His command on the Mauryan army started growing day by day and because of this, his elder brothers became suspicious of him being favoured by Bindusara as the next emperor. The eldest son of Bindusara, Prince Susima, convinced him to send Asoka to Takshashila province (in Sindh) to control an uprising caused by the formation of different militias. However, the moment Asoka reached the province, the militias welcomed him with open arms and the uprising came to an end without any fight. This particular success of Asoka made his elder brothers, especially Susima, more insecure.

Asoka went to Kalinga, where he met a fisherwoman named Kaurwaki. He fell in love with her and later, made Kaurwaki his second or third wife. Soon, the province of Ujjain started witnessing a violent uprising. Emperor Bindusara called back Asoka from the exile and sent him to Ujjain.

After ruling over the Indian subcontinent for a period of approximately 40 years, the great Emperor Asoka left for the holy abode in 232 BC. After his death, his empire lasted for just fifty more years.

93. PREM CHAND

An extremely famous name that comes to mind when we talk about Urdu novel writers is that of Prem Chand. The life history of Premchand is like that of any ordinary man. But what makes him stand out are the numerous works he composed in his lifetime. They are still read with much enthusiasm and admiration. Though he had financial crunches all through his life, he had the rich collection of his works and compositions.

Premchand was popularly known as Munshi Premchand and was one of the greatest literary figures of modern Hindi literature. His stories vividly portrayed the social scenario of those times.

Premchand's real name was Dhanpat Rai Srivastava. He was born on July 31, 1880 in Lamahi near Varanasi where his father Munshi Azayab Lal was a clerk in the post office. Premchand lost his mother when he was just seven years old and his father married again. Premchand was very close to his elder sister. His early education was in a madarasa under a Maulavi, where he learnt Urdu. When he was studying in the ninth class he was married, much against his wishes. He was only fifteen years old at that time.

Premchand lost his father when he was sixteen years old. Premchand was left responsible for his stepmother and step siblings. He earned five rupees a month tutoring a lawyer's child. Premchand passed his matriculation exam with great effort and took up a teaching position, with a monthly salary of eighteen rupees. While working, he studied privately and passed his Intermediate and B.A. examinations. Later, Premchand worked as the deputy sub-inspector of schools in what was then the United Provinces.

Premchand was a great social reformer; he married a child widow named Shivarani Devi. She wrote a book on him, 'Premchand Ghar Mein' after his death. In 1921 he answered Gandhiji's call and resigned from his job. He worked to generate patriotism and nationalistic sentiments in the general populace. When the editor of the journa *Maryaada* was jailed in the freedom movement Premchand worked for a time as the editor of tha journal. Afterward, he worked as the principal of a school in Kashi.

94. SAROJINI NAIDU

Sarojini Naidu was born at Hyderabad on February 13, 1879 and was the eldest of a large family, all of whom were taught English at an early age. At the age of twelve she passed the matriculation of the Madras University, and awoke to find herself famous throughout India.

Sarojini was a bright child who passed her matriculation at the age of 12, standing first in the Madras Presidency. She studied at the King's College, London, and Girton College, Cambridge for a while. During this period her creative urge found expression in poems. She also happened to be a good singer. Her ability to sing charmingly fetched her the title 'Nightingale of India'. After 1917 she stepped into active politics. In 1898 she married Dr. Govindarajulu Naidu.

Before she was fifteen the great struggle of her life began. Dr. Govindarajulu Naidu, later to become her husband was, though of an old and honourable family, not a Brahmin. The difference of caste roused an equal opposition, not only on the side of her family, but of his; and in 1895 she was sent to England, against her will, with a special scholarship from the Nizam. She remained in England, with an interval of travel in Italy, till 1898. She returned to Hyderabad in September 1898, and in the December of that year, to the scandal of all India, broke through the bonds of caste, and married Dr. Naidu.

In 1925, she chaired the Summit of Congress in Kanpur. In 1928, she went to the USA with the message of the non-violence movement from Gandhiji. When in 1930, Gandhiji was arrested for a protest, she took the helms of his movement. In 1931, she participated in the Round Table Summit, along with Gandhiji and Pundit Malaviyaji. In 1942, she was arrested during the "Quit India" protest and stayed in jail for 21 months with Gandhiji. After independence, she became the Governor of Uttar Pradesh. She was the first woman governor and passed away on March 2, 1949.

95. RABINDRANATH TAGORE

Rabindranath Tagore was born on May 7, 1861 in a wealthy Brahmin family in Calcutta. He was the ninth son of Debendranath and Sarada Devi. His grandfather Dwarkanath Tagore was a rich landlord and social reformer. Rabindranath Tagore had his initial education in Oriental Seminary School. But he did not like the conventional education and started studying at home under several teachers. After undergoing his Upanayan rite at the age of eleven, Tagore and his father left Calcutta in 1873 to tour India for several months, visiting his father's Santiniketan estate and Amritsar before reaching the Himalayan hill station of Dalhousie. There, Tagore read biographies, studied history, astronomy, modern science, and Sanskrit, and examined the classical poetry of Kalidasa.

In 1884, Tagore wrote a collection of poems *Kori-o-Kamal* (Sharp and Flats). He also wrote dramas - *Raja-o-Rani* (King and Queen) and *Visarjan* (Sacrifice). In 1890, Rabindranath Tagore moved to Shilaidah (now in Bangladesh) to look after the family estate. Between 1893 and 1900 Tagore wrote seven volumes of poetry, which included *Sonar Tari* (The Golden Boat) and *Khanika.* In 1901, Rabindranath Tagore became the editor of the magazine named *Bangadarshan.* He established Bolpur Bramhachary Ashram at Shantiniketan, a school based on the pattern of old Indian ashrama system. In 1902, his wife Mrinalini died. Tagore composed Smaran in her memory.

Rabindranath Tagore became the first Asian to become a Nobel laureate when he won Nobel Prize for his collection of poems, *Gitanjali,* in 1913. He was awarded Knighthood by the British King George V; and he established Viswabharati University.

Rabindranath Tagore was an icon of Indian culture. He was a poet, philosopher, musician, writer, and educationist. He was popularly called 'Gurudev' and his songs were known as Rabindra Sangeet. Two songs from his Rabindra sangit canon are now the National anthems of India and Bangladesh: the Jana Gana Mana and the Amar Shonar Bangla.

96. RANI LAKSHMI BAI

Rani Lakshmibai was one of the leading warriors of India's first struggle of independence. She is a symbol of bravery, patriotism and honour. She was born on 19th November, 1835, at Poona. Her father Moropant Tambe was a court advisor, and mother Bhagirathi was a scholarly woman. At a very early age she lost her mother. Her father raised her in an unconventional way and supported her to learn to ride elephants and horses and also to use weapons effectively. She grew up with Nana Sahib and Tatya Tope, who were active participants in the first revolt of independence.

In 1842, Rani Lakshmibai was married to Raja Gangadhar Rao who was the Maharaja of Jhansi. After her marriage to Gangadhar Rao she was called Rani Lakshmi Bai. In 1851, she gave birth to a son but unfortunately he died in his fourth month. After this tragic incident, Damodar Rao was adopted by The Maharaja of Jhansi as his son. Moved by the death of his son and his poor health, Maharaja Gangadhar Rao also died on 21st November 1853. When the Maharaja died, Rani Lakshmi Bai was just eighteen years old, but she didn't lose her courage and took up her responsibilities.

Lord Dalhousie, the Governor-general of India at that time, was a very shrewd person who tried to take advantage of the misfortune of Jhansi to expand the British Empire. The British rulers did not accept little Damodar Rao as the legal heir of late Maharaja Gangadhar Rao and Rani Lakshmi Bai. Their plan was to annexe Jhansi on the ground that it did not have any legal heir. In March 1854 Rani of Jhansi was granted an annual pension of Rs. 60,000 and was ordered to leave the Jhansi fort. She was firm on the decision not to give up the dominion of Jhansi to Britishers.

For strengthening the defense of Jhansi Rani Lakshmi Bai assembled an army of rebels, which also included women. For this great cause she was supported by brave warriors like Gulam Gaus Khan, Dost Khan, Khuda Baksh, Sunder-Mundar, Kashi Bai, Lala Bhau Bakshi, Moti Bai, Deewan Raghunath Singh and Deewan Jawahar Singh. She assembled 14,000 rebels and organized an army for the defense of the city. However, again a fierce battle took place and on the second day of fighting, at the age of 22 years, she lost her life, on 18th June 1858.

97. BAL GANGADHAR TILAK

Bal Gangadhar Tilak was born on July 22, 1856. He was universally recognized as the Father of Indian Unrest. He was one of the prime architects of modern India and heralded Asian nationalism. His philosophy could not survive after his death as India came under sway of Mahatma Gandhi.

Bal Gangadhar Tilak was a brilliant politician as well as a profound scholar who believed that independence is the foremost necessity for the well being of a nation and to win it through extreme measures should not be dispensed with. He was the first intellectual leader to understand the importance of mass support and subsequently became the first mass leader of India. He realized that the constitutional agitation in itself was futile against the British and, moreover, India was ill prepared for an armed revolt.

As a result, although he was helpful to revolutionaries such as Savarkar, Aurobindo Ghosh and Chaphekar, he did not venture into it himself. Instead, he martialled the extremist wing of Indian National Congress. His movement was based on the principles of Swadeshi, Boycott and Education.

It was he who, through his own example, gave prestige to imprisonment in freedom struggle. It is a tragedy that his work is not given the recognition due to it.

He was among the founders of the New English School, Pune (1881) of which Prof Chiplunkar became the Principal. He had a genius for organisation and with Agarkar, the then foremost social reformist, started the newspapers 'Kesari' and 'The Maratha' in 1881 and in 1890's started the annual celebration of 'Shivaji Festival' and 'Ganapati Festival' which served as a platform for people to join in the nationalist movement against the British. Unless Swaraj is obtained, India shall not prosper. It is necessary for our very own existence.

At 00:40 hrs on Aug 1, 1920, he was declared dead. It is said that the British made an extraordinary request that his brain be handed over to them so that it could be studied, preserved and exhibited. It was not complied with.

98. RAJA RAM MOHUN ROY

Raja Ram Mohun Roy (1774-1833) was the pioneer of modern thinking in India. A social reformer at heart, he greatly opposed orthodox practices that were prevalent in the Hindu society and relentlessly pursued progressive views. With a view to propagate his ideas and thoughts Roy founded the Brahma Samaj, an organization dedicated to expose the hypocrisies of the practitioners of religion.

Raja Ram Mohun Roy was born in a wealthy Brahmin family, at Hooghly in West Bengal. Though belonging to an orthodox family, he held modern views. He did not approve of the superstitions existing in the society. He greatly supported the English and Western styles of education. He was interested in the positive aspects of the European societies. He held the philosophies of democracy, liberalism and humanism in high regard.

Raja Ram Mohun Roy studied different religious systems including Christianity and Islam. The idea of monotheism preached by these religions greatly impressed him. He held the view that many practices followed by the Hindu society did not conform to the principles of real Hinduism. He attacked many evil practices in the Hindu society such as the caste system and child marriage. The most significant of his works, however, was the abolishment of Sati, a cruel practice of burning a widow on the pyre of her dead husband.

Apart from being a social reformer, Raja Ram Mohun Roy was also a scholarly person. He learned various languages such as English, Persian, Arabic, Latin, French and Hebrew. He was the master of his mother tongue Bengali and translated the Vedas and Upanishads into Bengali. Also, he established several newspapers and schools in variuous parts of India.

99. SWAMI VIVEKANANDA

A spiritual genius of commanding intellect and power, Vivekananda crammed immense labour and achievement into his short life. 1863-1902. Born in the Datta family of Calcutta, the youthful Vivekananda embraced the agnostic philosophies of the Western mind along with the worship of science. At the same time, vehement in his desire to know the truth about God, he questioned people of holy reputation, asking them if they had seen God. He found such a person in Sri Ramakrishna, who became his master, allayed his doubts, gave him God vision, and transformed him into a sage and prophet with authority to teach.

After Sri Ramakrishna's death, Vivekananda renounced the world and criss-crossed India as a wandering monk. His mounting compassion for India's people drove him to seek their material help from the West. Accepting an opportunity to represent Hinduism at Chicago's Parliament of Religions in 1893, Vivekananda won instant celebrity in America and a ready forum for his spiritual teaching.

For three years he spread the Vedanta philosophy

and religion in America and England and then returned to India to found the Ramakrishna Math and Mission. Exhorting his nation to spiritual greatness, he a wakened India to a new national consciousness. He died on July 4, 1902, after the second, much shorter sojourn in the West.

In addition, he delivered innumerable lectures, also wrote inspired letters in his own hand to his many friends and disciples, composed numerous poems, and acted as spiritual guide to the many seekers, who came to him for instruction. He also organized the Ramakrishna Order of Monks, which is the most outstanding religious organization of modern India. It is devoted to the propagation of the Hindu spiritual culture not only in the Swami's native land, but also in America and in other parts of the world.His lectures and writings have been gathered into several volumes.

100. V.S. NAIPAUL

V.S. Naipaul is a noble laureate who won Nobel Prize for Literature in 2001. Though of Indian origin, V.S. Naipaul was born in Trinidad and is currently a British citizen.

V.S. Naipaul (Sir Vidiadhar Surajprasad Naipaul) was born on August 17, 1932, at Chaguanas, Trinidad and Tobago. His forefathers came as indentured labourers from India. Naipaul's upbringing familiarised him with every sort of deprivation, material and cultural. He got a scholarship to Oxford University and thus came to England. It was at Oxford that V.S. Naipaul discovered the writer in him.

V.S. Naipaul travelled extensively in India and Africa. At that time decolonisation was taking place and Sir V.S. Naipaul observed from close quarters the resulting turmoil of emotions. These observations were reflected in his writings. V.S. Naipaul has written about slavery, revolution, guerrillas, corrupt politicians, the poor and the oppressed, interpreting the rages so deeply rooted in our societies.

V.S. Naipaul's fiction and especially his travel writing have been criticised for their allegedly unsympathetic portrayal of the Third World. But his supporters argue that he is actually an advocate for a more realistic development of the Third World. V.S. Naipaul's contempt for many aspects of liberal orthodoxy is uncompromising, but at the same time he has exhibited an open-mindedness toward some Third World leaders and cultures that isn't found in western writers.

V.S. Naipaul has discussed Islam in several of his books and he has been criticised for harping on negative aspects of Islam. V.S. Naipaul's support for Hindutva has also been controversial. He has been quoted describing the destruction of the Babri Mosque as a "creative passion", and the invasion of Babur in the 16th century as a "mortal wound."

V.S. Naipaul has won several awards and honours for his writings. In 1971, Naipaul won the Booker Prize for his book "In a Free State" and became the first person of Indian origin do so. He won the Jerusalem Prize in 1983 and Nobel Prize for Literature in 2001.

101. VED VYAS

The author of the great epic Mahabharata, Ved Vyas was the first and greatest acharya of Sanatan Dharma. He is responsible for classifying the four Vedas and wrote the 18 Puranas and recited the great Mahabharata. In fact, the Mahabharata is often called as the fifth Veda. Its most important and the most glorified section is the Bhagwad Gita, the lesson recited to Arjuna by Lord Krishna on the battlefield. The biography of Ved Vyas is very vivid and makes an interesting read.

Around some 5000 years ago, he was born on an island on the holy river Yamuna. His father was Parashar Rishi, a sage and his mother was Satyavati. He taught the Vedas to his pupils with ardent devotion and dedication. It is said that Mahabharata is the 18th Puran a that was written by Ved Vyas. He fathered four famous sons, Pandu, Dhritarashtra, Vidur and Shukdev. Ved Vyas received knowledge from great sages like Vasudeva and Sanakadik. He described that the most important goal in one's life was to attain Narayana or the Divine Supreme.

Apart from the Mahabharata, he also wrote the Brahma Sootra, one of his shortest theologies on Hindu philosophy. It is said that Ved Vyas is immortal and he never died. Seeing the widespread violence in today's times, he is said to have retreated into some remote village in Northern India. The life of Ved Vyas is an example to all in modern times on how to be selfless and devote oneself entirely to Lord in order to attain Nirvana.

Ved Vyas does not signify the name of any one person. It is a title. The author of the Mahabharata, is called 'Ved Vyas' because it was he who classified the Vedas into four branches. His hermitage was in Badari and he was therefore known as 'Badarayana'.

23.	School Essays & Letters for Juniors	75/-
24.	Common Mistakes in English	125/-
25.	The Power of Writing	150/-
26.	Learn English in 21 Lessons	125/-
27.	First English Dictionary	95/-
28.	Boost Your Spelling Power	125/-
29.	Self-Help to English Conversation	125/-
30.	The Art of Effective Communication	125/-
31.	A Book of Proverbs & Quotations	110/-
32.	Word Power Made Easy	125/-
33.	English Grammar Easier Way	125/-
34.	General English for Competitive Examinations	125/-
35.	Spoken English	125/-
36.	School Essays, Letters Writing and Phrases	95/-
37.	How to Write & Speak Better English	125/-
38.	Quote Unquote (A Handbook of Famous Quotations)	150/-
39.	Improve Your Vocabulary	125/-
40.	Common Errors in English	125/-
41.	The Art of Effective Letter Writing	125/-
42.	Synonyms & Antonyms	125/-
43.	Idioms	125/-
44.	Business Letters	110/-